Special Comments

"As a physician I believe in taking care of both your physical and emotional well-being. Patients tend to see their primary doctor when experiencing emotional symptoms. It is good practice to have resources available. *He Who First Held Her Heart* is an awesome resource, and so relevant in helping women in our communities to heal from the myriad of challenges resulting from being raised as fatherless daughters. Combining her professional credentials, spiritual beliefs, and life experiences, Sonja brings a unique quality to the subject of fatherlessness. This book will help fatherless daughters find their emotional peace as they navigate through this healing process. Throughout the book, Sonja becomes transparent as she shares her story, her own healing process, and words of encouragement. I will definitely recommend this great book to family and friends—and also keep copies in my exam rooms for my patients."

– Felicia Robertson, MD

"This book really helped me to realize "the traits of a victim" I carried in my marriage. I became aware of the emotional abuse that I was hiding in my marriage. I then knew that I was struggling with my self-worth."

–Anonymous

HE WHO FIRST HELD HER HEART

He Who First Held Her Heart Copyright © 2013 by Sonja P. Moore

FIRST EDITION

Published by GODSPEED Press, in Milwaukee, WI

Printed in the United States of America

All rights reserved. No part of this book and/ or cover may be reproduced or transmitted in any form or by any means without written permission from the author.

ISBN
978-0-9914998-0-9
978-0-9914998-1-6

Library of Congress Control Number: 2014934601

To order or for more information, contact us at:

414-627-9920

or visit: www.HeWhoFirstHeldHerHeart.com

FACEBOOK: He who first held her heart

Dedication

I dedicate this book to all fatherless daughters. I pray you find a "father figure," if your father continues to be unavailable. May God bring peace to both fathers and daughters as you work to mend your broken hearts. I hope this book can be used as a tool to help you repair your hearts and restore your relationship to a new beginning.

My heart especially goes out to the women who have succumbed to domestic violence, been sexually abused, and those who have suffered as a result of being fatherless. Thank you for sharing, and I pray you find your voice as you continue to embark on your own journey of self-discovery and healing.

Special dedication to my own father—for you are the reason I wrote this book. After our last conversation, I found myself back in my childhood, holding the fragile little girl who was first abandoned by her father. Our encounter helped me realize what I had been missing in my life. I did not write this book to blame you. I wrote it to show what the world was like through my eyes without you. I wish I could have had a closer relationship with you.

Table of Contents

Foreword v
Preface vii
Tribute ix
Acknowledgment x
Introduction xiii

Part I: Born into a Broken Heart
Chapter 1   What Happened to Daddy's Little Princess? 3
Chapter 2   This Journey Was Not by Choice 19
Chapter 3   Daddy, Where Did You Put My Crown? 37
Chapter 4   Letters to Their Fathers 47

Part II: Loving with Broken Heart
Chapter 5   Desperately in Search of 73
Chapter 6   A Woman without a Crown 85
Chapter 7   Not in Search of a King 97
Chapter 8   Am I Not Your Daughter? 113

Part III: Mending the Pieces
Chapter 9   In Search of Her Crown 129
Chapter 10 How Does She Forgive Him, and Them? 143
Chapter 11 She Crowns Herself Queen 155
Chapter 12 A Queen in Waiting 165

Part IV: Hearts Unbroken
Chapter 13 What's a Daddy to Do, and Mommy, Too? 179
Chapter 14 What About The Fallen Princess? 191
Chapter 15 Letters to Their Daughters 199
Chapter 16 Who Will Fill Those Empty Shoes? 215

Foreword

As a Christian therapist in the field of Marriage and Family Therapy, I have witnessed so many women whose lives have been devastated as a result of growing up fatherless. However, they have neither realized the impact, nor did they have a guide to healing until now. This topic has also been painfully neglected and minimized by the psychotherapeutic community. Sonja not only reveals the harsh truth of the effects of fatherlessness on daughters, and provides a roadmap to healing, but also presents a guide for fathers, mothers, extended family, and the community, to assist in mending the hearts and lives of those children born into a broken heart of fatherlessness.

Many fatherless daughters do not have self-worth, self-validation or self-love. Sonja points out as a result, these daughters try to find love and validation in desperation, which leads to their own detriment. These maladaptive behaviors provide fertile ground for the creation of abusive relationships in friendships, families, peers, and mates. These broken women subconsciously seek out this unfulfilled love in relationships that remind them of their fathers who were abusive and/or emotionally unavailable to them.

In her book *He Who First Held Her Heart*, Sonja Moore bravely reveals her own story of childhood trauma due to the abandonment of her father. Her father was to protect her and teach her self-worth, self-love, and self-validation, but he was not there for her. Without that foundation, she sought to meet her own needs to survive, doing so by hiding the truth behind a mask of confidence and academic success.

Her faith in God, along with her professional excellence as a Marriage and Family therapist, has allowed her to provide a roadmap both for the victims of fatherlessness, and those therapists who seek to help their clients find healing. Not only did Sonja reveal her own pain through her story, but she demonstrates her faith in God as he leads her on her journey. This book brings both emotional and spiritual enlightening, hope, wholeness, and forgiveness to those who travel the road she presents. It teaches women how to heal, love, and forgive themselves and others, as well as their absent father.

– Darlene B. Wareham, MS, LMFT, BCPCC

Preface

As a young girl, I longed for my father's love, but I never realized how his absence would lead me down a road of desperation—as I searched for love in all the wrong places. Just a few years ago, I was unable to face my painful truth so I brushed it off, put on "my mask," and pretended nothing in life bothered me. On the outside I was a strong woman envied by others, but inside I was losing the essence of myself as I exited one abusive relationship after the other. One day, my pain caught up with me as a result of an unpleasant encounter with my father forced me to face the truth about my brokenness. It was this familiar emotional abandonment by him that forced me to face the little girl that was abandoned by him years ago.

This book started out as a simple letter to my father, but it would be over a year before I could write him. Instead, God had another plan and I found myself going back and dealing with the root of my pain that had been buried for years. Before I could write to my father, I realized I needed some degree of healing in order to face the hurt caused by him. I prayed and wrote, and wrote and prayed. I had no idea then I'd be writing a self-help book for others or be where I am today. I just listened to God's voice and wrote. Soon I realized the purpose of this book was not just for me, but also for others—sharing my story would help other women heal and absent fathers who desire to reach out to their lost daughters..

I realized a fatherlessness epidemic is plaguing the nation, affecting all races, social classes, and genders. However, working in an urban school district, and in private practice, only intensified my passion. I discovered this epidemic was often the root of poverty, teen pregnancy, domestic violence, addiction, low achievement, gender issues, school dropout, low academic performance, sexual abuse, homelessness, suicidal ideation, human sex trafficking, and criminal activity. Instantly I wanted to understand the psychological effects of the fatherless epidemic as it relates to not only women in the urban community, but all women. My further research fascinated my curiosity. A strong correlation was clear between fatherlessness and many, if not all, of the at-risk behaviors listed above.

Not only does this book bring the fatherlessness epidemic to the forefront, it walks the reader through the step-by-step process of healing and forgiveness. It doesn't matter if you are a fatherless daughter or absent father, you will find healing and substantive steps to repairing relationships as you read through the chapters.

A Brother's Tribute

By Montré Jermaine Moore

I, too was born into a broken heart. Thirty-two years ago I opened my eyes for the first time in the Milwaukee County Hospital. My mother was a patient at the Milwaukee County Mental Health Complex, and my father was then a security guard employed by that very complex. It was difficult enough to grow up in the presence of a mentally ill mother, and to be fatherless, only intensified the tragedy.

I am the younger brother of Sonja Moore. My sister and I do not share a father, yet we share the pain and realization of what it means to be born into a broken heart. I have had a front-row seat to the remarkable life of Sonja Moore. I have witnessed my sister's many great accomplishments, while living behind what we call our mask, hiding our pain from the world. He Who First Held Her Heart is Sonja's riveting testimony that pulls the covers off the truth and the lasting effects of fatherlessness. By nothing less than the Devine propose and will of God, Sonja removes her mask and shares the story of her life and the pain of growing up without her father.

Through her pain and desire to be loved, Sonja poured herself into her studies, unaware at the time that God's plan for her life was one day she would tell her story, not for the shedding of tears, but for the breaking the cycle of pain felt by millions of fatherless daughters across the nation. He Who First Held Her Heart is not merely the story of the author's life, but it is also a roadmap to healing for those who were born into a broken heart. The author pairs her personal life experience with fourteen-plus years of working in the Milwaukee Public School system as a school counselor, accompanied by her five-plus as a licensed Marriage and Family Therapist, to walk the reader step by step through the process of forgiveness, healing, and self-love.

Acknowledgments

Thanks to my heavenly father for being the driving force of my life, giving me the courage to confront myself, and the ability to face the issues keeping me stuck. You were there for me when I failed to acknowledge your grace. You showed me who you are and who I can be through you. I give all praises to you.

Thanks to my brother, Montré, for walking on this difficult journey with me and encouraging me to share my story. Thanks for listening without judgment and allowing me to expose my pain. Words can't express my love and gratitude to you. Thank you for striving to be a present father to your daughter, even though you grew up without one. May God bless you as continue your growth stronger in him.

Thanks to my boys for your patience with my imperfections and for allowing me to steal your mommy moments to write this book. Your unconditional love and support is immeasurable.

Thanks to Tonyia, Alice, Natalie, Mollie, Caroline and the many people who were there and offering support. I love you all so much for the love and support you showed me, and also my sons. Thanks to my family and friends for listening to my experiences and offering comforting words or a shoulder to lean on. I don't have to name you, because you already know who you are. Much love to all of you.

Thanks to Dr. Felicia Robertson, Darlene Wareham, LMFT, BCCPC, and Kevin O'Brien, LMFT, LCSW for your professional critiques and community support.

A very special thanks to the participants for sharing your letters, being a subject in the photos, submitting father daughter photos, etc. Your words will provide healing to many who need to hear them.

All photos were done by "Photography by Amelia," 414-393-8333. Thanks so much Megan Hernandez-Tillmon for making my visions come to life. Your work is amazing.

Thanks to Kou Vang for designing such a beautiful cover and design.

Thanks to my editors Connie Anderson of Word & Deeds, Inc. and Carolyn Kott-Washburne. Thanks for the long hours of hard work. I appreciate your dedication and help in seeing this project get to the finish line.

I must also thank all of my coworkers at Transformations Learning Community (TLC) & Transition High Schools (THS) for being a listening ear during the periods of frustration, believing in my vision, giving words of encouragement, and advice. Thanks for being my extended family. You guys rock!

Introduction

When I began to write this book, I assumed its purpose was to bring into awareness the epidemic of the fatherless daughter and the impact it has on how she views her value in the world. However, as I came to the end of my own healing journey, I realized far more was at stake than how a woman views her value. I discovered a more devastating reality of which I was not aware. Not only does a fatherless woman have a distorted perception of her self-worth, she is more likely to become a victim of domestic violence, become a teen mother, engage in risk behaviors, become a mother of fatherless children, etc.

After I processed through my own personal journey, I encountered many fatherless daughters who shared similar stories, emotions, and difficulties as they sought help in processing through their childhood abandonment. I quickly realized this problem was much bigger than myself—and it affected at least one in four women in the United States.

This epiphany was both shocking and enlightened at the same time. It was the realization millions of heartbroken women are secretly struggling with abandonment, loneliness, and shame because they were never validated by their fathers. I consider myself an expert, as I have lived it, experienced it, and watched it fester within my own community. It's time for me to become transparent as I share my triumphs, tragedies, and revelations, revealing what it was like for me growing up as a fatherless daughter.

PART I:

Born into a Broken Heart

Chapter 1:
What Happened to Daddy's Little Princess?

Chapter 2:
This Journey Was Not By Choice.

Chapter 3:
Daddy, Where Did You Put My Crown?

Chapter 4:
Letters to Their Fathers

This section explains what it means to be fatherless and how fatherlessness affects children in the city of Milwaukee, as well as nationwide. It also addresses the raw issues young girls are likely to encounter as they grow up fatherless. In Chapter 2, I share my own personal journey as a fatherless daughter.

CHAPTER 1:

What Happened to Daddy's Little Princess?

A father should be the first man to hold his daughter's heart. When he captures her heart, she grows up knowing she is worthy of that kind of love.

What Happened to Daddy's Little Princess?

I couldn't stand the waiting as our late plane had finally arrived. The previous passengers began their exit. I moved closer and watched, as I mentally hurried them off. "Boy! Why is everyone moving so slow?" I accidentally blurted out as my mind raced ahead to my vacation destination. Suddenly I noticed her as she made her exit.

I quickly became distracted by her presence. She was a sweet little darling. From her tiny frame, she wasn't more than five or six years old. However, I could tell she was definitely someone's little princess, as she overwhelmed the scene with the plethora of pink. Everything was pink with the exception of the large, white and fluffy stuffed animal she was holding. Pink jacket, pink pants, pink shoes, and a tiny pink backpack to match. She resembled a delicate flower as everything stayed perfectly in place with the exception of a few unruly hairs. Then I noticed it: the large, blue tag dangling around her neck, which she tugged on as if it offered her added security. Her face was so precious, yet I could sense her fear as she exited the plane, escorted by the flight attendant. I witnessed the terror in her enormously large eyes as she scanned in search of something familiar. I was overcome with curiosity, because this was the first time I had seen a young child traveling alone. My concerns regarding our detained departure had become secondary, and for a brief second, I entertained this thought: "Who would send their precious little girl on a flight alone?"

Suddenly I could feel her mood shift, as her eyes lit up, and she yelled out excitedly, "Daddy!" "Daddy!" The flight attendant could no longer contain her as she broke the grip and dashed toward the man waiting for her. His face was beaming like the morning sun as he kneeled down, spread his arms, and engulfed her. When their eyes connected, they both released a gentle smile, sharing a common meaning, which defined the intimate bond between them. He kissed her repeatedly on her blushed cheeks as he gently stroked her hair with his strong hands. Within moments, he was up and standing, twirling around with her fragile frame buried beneath his grip. Soon they were off, and I watched their priceless image fade in the background. I could feel her excitement as her sweet voice carried on a rapid fire, one-sided conversation. "Daddy, I missed you so much." "Daddy, guess what?" "Daddy did you know that?" she said in the sweetest voice. I watched as he silently nodded with a smile, as if the voice in his ears was the most beautiful music he'd heard.

I felt like an intruder as I secretly studied their interactions and listened to their conversation. However, I couldn't help but wonder about their family dynamics. Was she coming from a visit with a relative, and he was just picking her up? Was there some custody agreement where she travels between her two parents in different states? None of these scenarios mattered. What mattered was the ongoing father-daughter connection between them. It was obvious they had a strong bond between them because it radiated throughout the space around them. This scene could have been captured in a movie, because it is more common to witness a young girl longing for her father than it is to see her being loved by him.

Although a grown woman, the little girl inside of me envied their interactions.

Many fatherless daughters grew up unaware they were lacking the crucial father-daughter connection needed as they navigated through the twists and turns of life from childhood into womanhood. When a father is not there to guide us, we are often left floundering. Instead of growing up feeling like a little princess, I grew up feeling abandoned, unloved, and unworthy of being loved. What led me on this journey of self-discovery was my desperation and need to be validated by my own father. Once we connected again when I was an adult, instead of getting the love and validation I needed from him, I often walked away feeling even more abandoned, unloved, and unworthy.

As I became aware of the daddy-daughter love I had spent a lifetime longing for, my life began to make sense. The more I began to work on healing the little broken girl within me, the more I found myself fixated on images of the intimate interactions between a father and daughter I saw around me. I recorded many of these interactions in my journal. I didn't realize at the time why I needed to record them; I assumed it was because I secretly longed to be that little girl.

All little girls aspire to capture their father's heart. As early as three years old, a little girl begins to recognize her self-worth through the eyes of her father and begins to seek approval from him. For example, a young toddler may prance around her daddy in her new dress so he can tell her she looks beautiful. When she grows up feeling loved, secure, and valued by her father—in her adult relationships, she will seek the standard of love she had with him.

If she does not have a father present, she becomes aware of his absence as she watches others around her. She may be too young to make sense of what she is lacking. However, as she grows older, there comes a critical time when this little girl really needs her daddy, and something in her innately searches for that daddy-daughter relationship. In the eyes of a little girl, no other love can supersede a daddy's love. When such love is absent, the love she must have for herself becomes displaced. In his absence, this longing for him festers as she struggles through life, trying to make sense of who she is. She begins to replace her dreams of him loving her with the reality of her lack of self-worth, self-esteem, and self-love.

A father who is committed to the emotional well-being of his little princess will be there to protect, love her, and help guide her through life, even if he no longer has love for her mother. What happened to Daddy's little princess? This is a serious question, because for every little girl who knows she is her daddy's little princess, three or four little girls only dream of being a princess.

It's no secret: millions of children in America are growing up without their fathers. I could have written about all of the statistics, because I did do my research. However, I wanted to keep it simple, because I know if you yourself did not grow up fatherless, you come in contact with children and adults who were. Society cannot keep turning away from the brutal fact that many young girls are suffering from lack of self-worth, self-esteem, and self-love. Without a father to validate her sense of self, she grows up feeling ashamed, abandoned, and unvalued.

As her view of herself becomes distorted, she will seek situations falsely mimicking the validation of her father. No matter how well she is groomed by her mother, it is her father whom she will seek the stamp of approval. It is only through his eyes she gains an understanding of her value and placement in the world as a woman. If she is validated in a healthy relationship with him, she is less likely to engage in risky behaviors, including criminal activity, drug or alcohol abuse, teen pregnancy, suicide, sexual exploitation of herself, or becoming a victim of domestic violence.

Again, I must ask, "What happened to daddy's little princess?"

As I look back at my youth, which was the 1970s and 1980s, it was obvious the role of a father had not yet faded during my generation. Despite the wave of divorce, and the acceptance of single motherhood invading our society, young girls would still dream of being daddy's little princess. Although our daddies were becoming absent in our homes during the '70s, we were still connected to the ideal of being daddy's little princess, and we were well aware of the princess crown. How could we forget? Fathers were seen as superheroes, men of wisdom filled with courage, and the one who knew how to fix any situation. No matter where we looked, we were surrounded by the strong daddy images through most of the popular TV shows, such as The Cosby Show, The Brady Bunch, Good Times, Family Matters, Family Ties, and the various other family-oriented shows demonstrating the important role a father played in his daughter's life. This role was also displayed in the media, in church, and in the homes of the many little girls who we knew as daddy's little princess.

We watched with envy as they danced their daddy-daughter dance, sang their daddy-daughter songs, and played their daddy-daughter games. However, with the 1980s, came a rise in teen pregnancy, signaling the beginning of a major shift in the expectation of the father's role. Because many of these teen moms were now first- and second-generation fatherless daughters, it was becoming common—a mother would be expected to raise a child on her own. However, back in the sixties, a fatherless home was almost unheard of. As society became aware of this growing epidemic, more programs surfaced in efforts to educate teens about birth control and unplanned pregnancies. I'm not sure how effective these programs are or if they teach both boys and girls to be responsible parents. Nevertheless, it appears that the responsibility is typically left in the hands of the teen mom.

Welfare and the demise of the nuclear family

With the false sense of security welfare brought in the '70s, the role of the father was being diluted in many impoverished homes. A family in need could not receive assistance if a father or any man was in the house. Many women in poverty learned quickly they could rely on welfare, as the role of their children's father was on the way to being eliminated. It has continued on as a repeated cycle where girls without daddies become mothers without husbands, who have girls without daddies, who then again become mothers without husbands, Etc. In some of the most impoverished areas, the mere reflection of the father-daughter's bond is like a faint light burning in the darkest night. It has not yet burned out, but still remains weakened as many communities have become accustomed to extinguishing the traditional family.

Through the wave of teen pregnancy, divorce, and acceptance of single motherhood, one has to wonder if the father's role will one day be eradicated. Although welfare has now become unreliable, this epidemic keeps little girls disconnected and desensitized to the role of a father altogether. As a result, she may have lost the meaning of the title "Daddy's little princess", and even the dream of one day becoming the Princess Bride. In exchange for her crown, society has pushed her into a role of self-exploitation as she mimics the negative images of women who came before her. However, this role fails to satisfy her innate desire to seek her daddy's approval.

As the nuclear family becomes more extinct, the fatherlessness epidemic is no longer contained inside of the inner city. It has affected the middle class, upper-middle class, blacks, whites, and all other ethnics groups. It is not unusual for daughters from two very different walks of life to share the same feelings of abandonment and unworthiness left by an absent father. There are even circumstances where, a daughter reports her father does live in the home, yet she grows up feeling emotionally fatherless. This is often the physically present but emotionally absent father. Later in the chapter I will go more in depth as I define the four father-daughter relationship models.

A validating survey

A father's role is crucial in his daughter life —and she is unable to grow up emotionally intact without him. To prove this fact, I felt compelled to search for research on fatherlessness, particularly fatherless daughters. I wanted to make sure I was able to validate what I had begun to discover. I found tons of research on the effects of fatherlessness, and was taken aback by the strong correlations. Those facts were not sufficient enough, because I needed to prove myself right.

Thus, I created a twenty-two question survey centering on my interests. The first seven questions were basic identifying questions so I was able to establish my two groups (fatherless versus those who had fathers). For example: What is your race? How old are you? Did you grow up with your father? The other 15 questions were very direct and required a yes or no answer or a short response. For example: Did you feel loved by your father? Were you sexually active as a teenager? Were you a victim of domestic violence? Were you a teen mom? Did you ever hate yourself?

If they answered "yes" to the question, they were given 1 point. A higher score meant they were admitting to engaging in risky behaviors, etc. The complete survey can be found in the back of the book. I surveyed over 150 random women from all ethnic backgrounds, social economic statuses, and ranging between ages 16 and 65.

What I found was a strong correlation between absent fathers and negative feelings about self, suicide, teen pregnancy, drug and alcohol use, sexual abuse, and domestic violence. Daughters who felt they were fatherless had a much higher score than daughters who felt their relationship with their father was intact. Race, age, and religion were not a significant factor. I realize all fatherless daughters may not suffer severe emotional effects as a result of their absent fathers. In some cases, fatherless daughters grow up emotionally intact, and may appear to have little to no effects from being fatherless. However, I'm not sure how they manage to figure out how to find their sense of self without their father. This is rare, because the major damage is done before they are even aware of it. By the time it's discovered, many fatherless girls have been subjected to repeated abandonment, sexual abuse, and self-exploitation. The unfortunate fact is many fatherless daughters have perished as the result, and many of these cases have gone unnoticed.

Along with my own personal journey, I've had the privilege of providing services to other fatherless daughters who were also on their journey in search of their own validation as they heal from fatherlessness. As a result of the combination of my own story, other stories, my professional experience, and my own research, I came up with my own relationship models in order to explain my discoveries. These are not diagnoses you will find recorded in The Diagnostic and Statistical Manual of Mental Disorders, Fourth Edition (DSMIV). Please note: the models are used to describe the various types of father-daughter relationships.

In addition to models, I will often refer to the phase "born into a broken heart." Born into a broken heart simply means when a child is being raised without the presences of one or both parents, the mere abandonment exposes them to emotions that would later affect who they love, how they love, and who they become. Later in the book I will refer to the phrase "loving in a broken heart."

Loving in a broken heart is a phrase use to describe an emotionally broken people's distorted view of love.

Some fathers are physically and emotionally absent by no choice of their own. This can be due to traumatic events such as severe illness, death, active duty, etc. Please note I uphold the highest respect for these situations, as I understand this father has not chosen to be physically and/or emotionally absent. Yet their daughters are not excluded, as they experience many of the same emotions as they seek to validate their sense of self. It is also possible for these daughters to find healing in this book, as there are familiar feelings as a result of the mere loss of a father, i.e., grief, loneliness, sadness, anger, and even abandonment.

However, in these models my focus is on the physically and/or emotionally absent fathers, absent by choice. These are fathers who become absent through divorce and/or separation from the mother, and make no attempt to remain physically and/or emotionally present in their daughter's life.

Father-daughter relationship models

Based on my professional knowledge of parenting, I have created four models to define my interpretation of father-daughter relationships. Before explaining these models, I think it is necessary to give a description of what I consider to be an absent father. When I refer a father's absence, I am not solely referring to the physical absence of a father. I am referring to the physical and/or emotional absence, because both are equally devastating. In my opinion, it is almost impossible for a daughter to fully develop emotionally without both the physical and emotional presence of her father. In rare cases where they do, there is still a great impact caused by her father's absence.

There are four types of father-daughter relationship models I feel are most significant. I will go through each of the models and give a detailed description. I understand it is not possible to include all father-daughter relationship dynamics within my models. As it is clear, some situations overlap or may not be defined. Below is a description of the following models I have composed to help readers define their own father-daughter relationship. Here are the acronyms of the listed models Physically/Emotionally Present: PEP, Physically/Emotionally Absent: PEA, Physically Absent/ Emotionally Present: PAEP, and Physically Present/ Emotionally Absent: P-PEA. As you read about the different models, see which one best fits your father-daughter relationship.

1) Physically /Emotionally Present: PEP

I would be the first to acknowledge the many fathers who deserve the "father of the year" award. Over the last three years, I have secretly watched fathers engage with their daughters in various settings. I have watched at restaurants, in the parks, at the zoo, etc. Whenever I captured a daddy-daughter interaction, I studied it. I discovered many fathers are aware of the important role they play in their baby girl's life. While at work, I have had the privilege of listening to the men boast and brag about the cute comments, funny mishaps, major accomplishment of daddy's little princess. Just by ease dropping on their conversations, I know that these gloating fathers were not only physically present, but emotionally present as well.

A PEP father is defined as a father who fully accepts his role, as he is both physically and emotionally present.

- Although he realizes the importance of having a physical presence in his daughter's life, as it is essential to tend to her financial needs, he is also aware of his daughter's need for love, self-worth, and validation.
- He makes every attempt possible to fulfill his role in her emotional development. He is available to her as she navigates through life in search of herself.
- He understands she looks to him to define her role in society as girl, woman, wife, etc.
- Even if he and the mother are not together, he still accepts his role as a father and understands the equal responsibility of parenting.

- If he is local, he will do whatever he can to assure there is a workable custody arrangement where he has physical interactions with his daughter on a regular ongoing basis.
- If his resides in another state, he still has regular communication and sets a visitation schedule working around the child's schedule to assure her emotional and physical interaction remains intact.
- He will chase away the invisible monster, be a dress-up playmate, tuck her in at night, listen to her imaginary stories, take her to all of her girly events, and engage in the many endless father daughter talks.
- He will assure his daughter always feels protected, safe, secure, loved, and validated.

As a result of his unconditional love, he captures her heart and becomes the first man she falls in love with. As she grows up, she develops a secure sense of self-worth and self-value, as she knows her daddy's heart lies in the palm of her tiny hands. Her gentle smile could wiggle her of any scolding, or could convince Daddy to read her just one more story. As she becomes a woman, she will later seek a man who mirrors her father's image. If she encounters a man who threatens her sense of self, she will not receive him, because she will look for the man to treat her like her father did.

2) Physically/Emotionally Absent: PEA

A PEA father is both physically and emotionally absent. Although many fathers aspire to be the best dads they can be, a large number of absent fathers may not have given fatherhood much thought. As parents, we sometimes carry around our own emotional baggage, and it can inhibit our ability to care for our children. For whatever reason, some fathers allow their daughters to grow up without having any physical or emotional involvement in their lives. As I mentioned earlier, in some cases this tragedy is unavoidable. In this model, I am referring to fathers who exit by choice. Sometimes the relationship with their child's mother just doesn't work out. The PEA father leaves his own children when he leaves the "Baby Mama." He allows years to pass without ever attempting to reconnect with his children.

As a mother, I am not able to understand how an absent father or mother chooses to walk away from their children. I remember hearing somewhere that men don't always connect with their children because they lack the maternal bond. I'm not so sure if I agree. Why, because I have interviewed men who are as invested in their children as any mother would be. In fact, many would seek joint custody if they were in a situation where they had to leave. Therefore, I can't help but wonder if those who choose to leave ever understood what life would be like for their little girl growing up without them.

In my professional opinion, having provided services for many of these little girls, it is equally devastating for a girl to grow up without her father as it is for a boy to grow up without his father.

- Young girls are more fragile because of their innate need to be protected, loved, and cared for. As a child, she looks to her father; as a woman she will seek it out in her mate. The mere reality of being fatherless is painful in itself, and it radiates a message promoting shame, guilt, and worthlessness.
- If this young girl knows her father has other children who he is present with, she feel even more unwanted and unworthy of his love. This damage is sometimes not repairable by anyone other than her father.
- She often blames herself or feels something she did caused her daddy to not love her.
- She may resent the siblings who have had the privilege of receiving such love from him.
- It is her relationships with her father that ensures self confidence and self-worth, and will enable her search for a healthy relationship. Otherwise she will engage in reckless relationships as she blindly chases to fill the void left by her father.

3) Physically Absent/Emotionally Present: PAEP

In today's society 50 percent of marriages are likely to end in divorce. When families break up, it is not unusual for one or both of the involved parties to decide to relocate. In addition to the difficulties of divorce, the children are left to follow a visitation schedule, which could mean they won't have physical contact with the other parent for long periods. This can leave a daughter feeling abandoned and neglected during the periods when her father is absent. For example, let's say a father has joint custody of his daughter, but only gets her for the summer months because he lives in another state. Although they have limited physical contact, he understands he is still her emotional father during his physical absence.

PAEP father is a father who may not be physically present all of the time, but still maintains an emotional presence in his daughter's life.

- This may be a father who is away due to active military duty, or he may reside in another state due to employment, or divorce. However, he makes every attempt to establish a strong emotional bond.

- Although this father has limited physical contact and activity, he reminds his daughter that his presence is very real. For example: he regularly sends her unexpected "surprise" packages, love notes, post cards and pictures..

- With today's technology, he has many resources as his disposal, for example Skype, Facebook, phone conversations, text messaging, Instagram, and email. Although it may not be the ideal way of interacting, it is a way for a father to show his love for his daughter.

- He also attempts to be physically present in his daughter's life whenever possible. If her mother is in agreement, he schedules unannounced visits whenever possible, and stays involved in the parenting of her and important decisions.

When I interviewed community agencies in my area, I discovered several programs where fathers who are in prison can still participate as active parents. I interviewed a former inmate who had spent twenty years in prison, and was able to take part in a fatherhood program that allowed regular visits and communication with his children. Although there were still many challenges as a result of his prison stay, his emotional connection with his children played a crucial role in their outcome and emotional development.

4) Physically Present/ Emotionally Absent: P-PEA

The emotionally absent father is sometimes unaware of the emotional bond needed between a father and daughter. Although he may be physically present, there is little or no emotional connection between them. It could be he is consumed with his career, or simply repeating the role his father filled during his childhood. There are still families who believe the father's role is to simply provide, while the mother cares for the children's emotional needs. This family may appear to be the typical nuclear family. However, the children grow up with the physical presence of a father, yet they too can grow up feeling fatherless. I'm not saying that this is always a typical situation. However, I am saying there are some fathers who are physically present, but are emotionally absent.

These daughters often develop similar characteristics as the daughter of a PEA father. However, what can harm her most are the daily reminders she has of a father who is there in her presence, yet is emotionally unavailable. After several unsuccessful attempts to get her father's attention, she usually starts to withdraw from her family as she secretly resents him. The resentment intensifies, as she convinces herself her daddy really doesn't care. In many instances, she may deliberately rebel against his authority because she is somewhat aware of the emotional abandonment. However, her actions causes her to feel even more invisible and unloved as she watches her daddy, who is clueless, until she decides to do something that is sure to get his attention.

The P-PEA is a father who is physically present, but has cemotionally abandoned his daughter.

- Despite the daily interactions, he is not emotionally available. There may be a strained relationship in which they have little-to-no communication between them.

- The father may be overly consumed with his work or his own emotional baggage, which take priority over their father-daughter bond.

- He may think he is connecting because he is a provider, establishes rules, and has a daily physical presence.

- In some cases, this father may battle substance abuse, is a workaholic, or may have unresolved issues from his own childhood.

Through the four models, you should be able to get a picture of the various father-daughter interactions. These are simply models based solely on my professional experience through interviews, surveys, and observations. They are not intended to be used to attack fatherhood, but are intended to outline what it means to be physically and emotionally absent.

I am not denying the physical and emotional absence of a mother has its own devastating effects. I believe it does. However, I am not prepared to comment on it at this time but I will strongly consider doing further research on the topic. If you know a father who is currently absent, please encourage him to make himself available to his children so the fatherlessness cycle is broken. It is never too late to love, protect, and validate your daughter. You may not be able to change the past, but you can have a great impact on her future.

In the next chapter, I will take you along on my journey through my childhood. I share my own experience and some of my most heartbreaking memories as a young girl who grows up longing for her father's love. On the outside, one would never imagine what you are about to learn about my past because through the years, I learned to mask my pain. However, the consequences of growing up without my father resulted in a repeated cycle of broken-heart syndrome. It took years for me to realize I was suffering from the lack of validation missing as a result of my father's absence.

CHAPTER 2

This Journey Was Not by Choice

How Can I Call You Daddy?

How can I call you Daddy when my life you never knew?

*How can I call you Daddy when my tears swelled
for you like the morning dew?*

*How can I call you Daddy when my fears went unattended,
and my wounds are not mended?*

I don't know how to pretend.

*I wish I understood this mysterious word,
but it's absent from my tongue.*

*How could it explain who you are, or
where in my life you belong?*

*How can I call you Daddy when the word has no meaning,
yet your love I've been feigning.*

*But, you were nothing more than a mysterious being,
how can I call you what...?*

I can hear it ring loudly as it yells at my pain.

How can I call you daddy when I only knew your name?

How can I call you anything other than your first name?

For many years, I was emotionally stuck in this vicious cycle because I was trying to find love in a broken heart. Most of my life, I was disconnected from the reality that I had grown up as a fatherless daughter. In order to understand why I kept getting stuck, I needed to revisit my childhood, and face the trauma I had experienced. However, God would not allow me to write this book any other way—until I released all of what was hidden deep within me. Initially, I tried to write this book without sharing my own personal story. I never thought I would have the courage to face what I am about to reveal, so I walked away from this project for almost a year.

One evening while I was enjoying the African World Festival, an older stranger joined us at our table. She said, "God knows what you have been through, and this time when you walk through your pain, know that he is with you. He is waiting for you to share your testimony, because there are so many hurting women who will find their deliverance from it." How did she know I was writing a book—and I was stuck? I trusted God, and I knew it was time to share my story.

In the seventies, Milwaukee, Wisconsin was a city where opportunities were blooming. My parents were young and inexperienced, yet they seemed to have had life figured out. Here I am, born Sonja P. Moore, baby girl number three. I was barely four pounds, my head was covered with sandy brown hair, and I was a mirror image of my father. The two little girls who came before were barely out of diapers, and still too young to occupy their own time. Later I would carry the burden of looking like my father, and living in his shadow.

At the time of my birth, my mother was 18-year-old and should have been graduating high school. However, she was a housewife, already a mother of two, and now a mother to a sickly newborn. Her married life contradicted her upbringing, because she grew up as the youngest of seven children in a strong Christian family. When she was five, her parents migrated to Wisconsin from the South in search of a better life. Although she grew up with her father, I can speculate from Grandma's stories he was emotionally absent. He was very involved in the church, had many medical issues, and suffered from severe diabetes, eventually leading to his untimely death when my mom was barely sixteen. My grandma also shared stories about his uneasy temperament and fits of rage. I can only imagine what life was like for my mother as a child. Perhaps this is what led her down her very own personal journey of loving in a broken heart.

My father was a muscular, 21-year-old man who stood well over six feet tall. As a little girl, I viewed him an enormous giant, yet I sometimes felt his gentle side. I believe he was born in Milwaukee, Wisconsin, and was the younger of two boys; his brother seventeen years his senior. I do not know a lot about my father's upbringing except he grew up in a two-parent home—and my grandfather was an alcoholic. I can only assume this impacted him as a young child. When I was in college, I spent time with my grandparents and experienced the alcohol abuse firsthand.

From the stories I was told, it appeared my parents were doing very well for themselves. Despite their young age, on the outside others envied them. They appeared together, lived in a nice house, worked their way up to the middle class, and took pride in taking care of us. We were the little girls who wanted for nothing, at least not anything materialistic. Soon life for my parents was not as easy as it had once seemed to be. Privately, inside our home, my parents were dealing with many issues—rumors of other women, my father's alcohol and drug use, his physical abuse, and a son from another woman. The mere fact my half-brother exists, confirms a betrayal of trust within my parents' marriage. Behind closed doors, we were now four little girls living in terror. We were too young to understand why our mother was being beaten. However, as a result we were depleted of our self-worth before we could even embrace it. I was told despite how horrible he treated my mother, my father adored his little girls. This gives me little comfort because of the fact that he later left, as well as the memories of my mother's abuse, contradict it.

Unpleasant memories of my father

Things were often unpredictable. I can still capture a quick moment of the physical violence corrupting our family. I can hear the echoes of my mother's screaming as it clouded my thoughts. My playtime would suddenly be interrupted by my mother's fear and panic. We never knew what to expect from him, yet I had become familiar with the clues, and knew immediately what to do. I learned to recognize the sounds of commotion and screams of terror as my signal to hide. My mother hid us in a closet, or in one of the drawers of the old, brown armoire standing like a large statue in the corner of our dining room. I was young, but somehow I knew when something was about to happen. As my father exploded in rage, he would yell, scream, and strike my mother.

I don't have many visual memories because my mother tried to protect us, so I didn't see many of the beatings—but I heard them. However, she failed to realize the escaping terror penetrated our innocent ears. I could still hear her voice overtaken by fear, and my father's voice fueled with rage. Hearing yelling, screaming, glass breaking, and dogs barking, my ears were too young to make sense of all this noise holding me in terror. In the aftermath, my wounded mother would treat her bruises as my father disappeared, until he resurfaced again hours, and sometimes days later.

The last visual memory I can recall of my father was when I was three years old. We were taking family photos, and my sisters and I were all lined up waiting to each have a photo taken alone with my father. I remember standing at the end of the line behind my three sisters, waiting my turn. I was afraid to approach the large, powerful frame sitting in the brown chair. My heart raced as I approached him. This was my father, yet I feared him. I stood in front of him as he invited me to join him in the chair. I waited for him to pick me up and place me firmly on his lap. My small, fragile frame sank in his lap as we sat in the large, brown leather chair and prepared for our pose. We were all dressed to impress those who got to see only our outer shell. Fear raced through my body as his large hands grabbed me around my narrow shoulders. He pointed at the camera, hoping I would release a smile the photographer was seeking. I could feel my body stiffen as he held me. I feared him because I had become familiar with the darkness dwelling within him, yet a part of me needed love from him.

I had no idea this day would be my only positive memory of his in my childhood. Was my birth the turning point for this young couple, or the birth of my baby sister while I was still in diapers? My baby sister was about a year old when my father finally decided to leave our family, and she has no childhood memories of him.

My mother's pain becomes more familiar. Although I was young, I can still recall the sadness in her eyes as she pretended she enjoyed our "happy" life. My mom was sad, yet she struggled to keep the reality of our life hidden from us. Only twenty, she was raising four young daughters alone. Our financial situation quickly changed, and we were now living in poverty. My mother went on welfare, moved into public housing, and tried her best to provide for her young daughters. As she became more frantic and financially unstable, she knew she needed help and went to her mother for refuge.

Grandma intervenes

Then one day my grandmother showed up and became a strong presence in our life. She had replaced my father, and I no longer had the opportunity to inquire about him. Without ever saying good-bye, my daddy was gone. Sometimes I wondered if my daddy would return. I wanted him to come back, yet I was afraid of him. Soon I was old enough to realize my father was not returning. No one ever said a word to us about my father again, and I was forced to mourn my father's absence in silence. In my mother's presence, I pretended she was all I needed, but I secretly missed my father. I lost a father but I gained a Big Mama. With my grandma's presence, I learned about God, and how I could rest my cares in him.

My mother was destined to put the pieces together so she could maintain our status in life. She went back to school, attended college, found full-time employment, and paved the way for her daughters. She became devoted to her faith, and church became her rescue, as it was a way to escape the pain residing outside of it. In my father's absence, her voice became my pacifier. I adored my mom, and wished I could hear her sing again. "It will be early," she would sing. The memory of watching my mother perform in various churches brings peace to my soul.

As we grew older, she dressed us all up in pretty lace dresses with matching hair bows, and trained the four of us to be her backup singers. She would spend hours practicing the many songs, some she had written herself. This was the highlight of my childhood, and the holidays brought out even more of the best of her. I remember waking up on Christmas morning to the many surprises under the tree. I could still smell the scent of the freshly baked coconut cake, and the candied ham in the oven. Although my dad wasn't there, my mom did her best to implant happy memories. I truly adored her, because we knew she loved us. Her staged joy and happiness prevented her from displaying the emptiness and deep sadness she must have carried in the absence of my father. She never allowed herself to grieve the abuse and loss of her marriage because she learned to carry her pain behind her mask.

As time went on, I watched as my mother began to struggle with her faith, as she tried her best to resemble the image of her mother. When I was seven, it had become obvious to everyone my mother had fallen out of faith with the Lord. She was in her mid-twenties, and had never had the opportunity to live as a young woman should. Despite my grandma's disapproval, my mother started dating and going out with friends outside of church. In the beginning, she tried to use her faith as her strength when she began to fall from grace. However, our life was quickly changing because she was not taking us to church anymore. At this point, Grandma's presence faded from our home, and she would only come to get us ready and take us to church.

One day my mom went out on a date, and we were left with an older cousin. I was excited about my mom dating because I thought it meant I would finally have another daddy. There was something different about this date. The evening was growing late, Mom was not home, and we were beginning to worry. This time I went to bed worried because I was not able to say good night. The next morning we woke to my mom's absence as we were being transported to Grandma's house. When we arrived, Grandma was surrounded by distraught family members, as well as several police officers. I was terrified when we were immediately escorted to the back room. I tiptoed to the front room to eavesdrop in order to make sense of what was going on. Grandma's face was rippled with worry, and I knew she was troubled.

After the first day, the excitement of my mother's absence faded, and many of the family members returned to their daily routines. However, those moments in my life remain at a standstill. Days went by, and my mother was nowhere to be found. In my heart, I was afraid I had lost my mom. Grandma refused to doubt her faith as she engaged in the daily rituals of prayer for her daughter's safe return. She was sure to include us as she instructed us each morning and evening to kneel by the window. "Pray and ask the Lord to bring Mama home," she would say, trying to disguise her voice of distress. "Please Lord bring my mother home." We would all cry out as we looked down the road expecting her to suddenly appear. I was now deeply saddened by the reality right then, I did not know where either of my parents were.

After days of worry and distress, I was filled with excitement because Mom was finally home. My joy quickly faded as I did not get the response I expected. Something about her was different, and the loving mother who cared for us was gone. She was completely out of it, appeared empty and disconnected, and didn't recognize we were in the room. It was as if something had stolen her soul. She stumbled into the doorway wearing a distorted version of the outfit she wore on her date, carrying her shoes in one hand. Looking in her eyes, I could not connect with her. She appeared to be my mother, but in my heart I could not receive her. My mother appeared cold, distant, and absent as we all stood around, confused. "Get back and give your mother some room," Grandma said as we were quickly shuffled in the back room to wait.

The first night, no one slept. My mother's presence disrupted the house. She was lost in complete madness as the reality of her trauma was trying to surface. She paced the floor and repeatedly interrupted Grandma's sleep in an effort to seek comfort for the madness she held within. I tried to sleep as the screams of terror invaded my dreams. My mother would become violent as we tried to make sense of the jargon she uttered repeatedly. By morning, we all suffered from exhaustion, and Grandma realized my mother needed help beyond her ability.

My mom was transported to the mental health hospital, where she remained for several months. After her first stay, she developed a pattern where she would cycle in and out as she struggled to regain her life. From then on, my mother stopped ever being the same again, and she never told anyone exactly what happened. This has been a big family secret no one wanted to speak about. However, I couldn't understand why everyone stood in silence while my mother became lost in her terror. My mother was never strong enough to come out of her madness.

When I became an adult, I discovered when my mother was out on the date, the guy drugged, kidnapped, and raped her. After keeping her for several days, he decided to let her go.

Over the next several years, my life was like a rollercoaster ride, and life with Mom was now too unstable. What remained of my happy life were the happy moments I had with her before she became ill. One moment we were with Mom, the next moment we were with Grandma while my mom sought treatment. There were long periods where she seemed well, and others where she needed long periods of hospitalizations. This woman who was struggling to care for me was not the mom I had watched singing in church. She lost her voice when she lost her mind.

We knew when she was going to have an onset. Despite how hard Mom tried to pull it together, it was obvious her mental illness would overtake her. The terror dwelling within her forced us to immediately awaken, and she would make us walk several miles in the middle of the night. We were all too young to understand why we needed to get out of bed, but we knew when she said let's go, we had to go. We would walk from one person's house to the next. When she was sick she was paranoid and withdrawn from us. She would often accuse us of trying to bring harm to her. Because I looked a lot like my father, she associated me my father and his abuse.

We all coped with my mother's illness in our own way. Life with her was sometimes unpredictable, and the reality of being fatherless became too intense to conceal. I missed my father, and I secretly cried for him at night. I wanted to escape, and I knew he was out there somewhere. I needed him to come rescue me from my mother's madness. I felt guilty for missing him, and for wondering what life would be like if he had never left us. Although it was hard, I had accepted the fact my mother would never be normal again, and I made peace with her illness. I then became fixated on the possibility of going to be with my daddy. I was ten when I asked my grandma about the possibility of going to live with my father. I was told he didn't mean us any good and had another family to take care of.

My Grandma kept us in church, and I found relief there. Although I enjoyed church, it was no longer the place where I could go to hear my mother sing. I now looked forward to secretly gazing at the images of the many church families. I paid close attention to the fathers who attended with their daughters. I was amused by their well-groomed, fancy suits, the colorful shades of brown skin, and the strong smell of the mixture of men's cologne that flooded the pews.

My visual image of my biological father had long faded as years had passed since my last sight of him. I gathered the beautiful images of the fathers loving their daughters, and stored them in my memory. I would reconstruct these images in my head, creating an image of an emotional daddy. I would dream of an imaginary castle, and my father, the handsome king who turned into a magic dragon when it was time to fight the bad monsters. In order to fall asleep at night, I would imagine myself being held tightly as I nestled in his arms. This imaginary closeness became an emotional escape, and kept me from the insanity of my reality. I would visit with him in my dreams, and he would wipe away my tears.

Sometimes the dreams felt so real, when I awoke, I could still feel the presence of my imaginary father. It was easy to get lost in the imaginary world I had created because I could go there to escape my trauma. This was the only place where I would go to spend time with "my father", and feel protected by him. I would go there for hours until something or someone on the outside forced me to come back. As a result, I became very introverted, and barely spoke to anyone on the outside. I became a target and was teased at school because I acted weird, but at home I was taunted because I looked the most like my father. The older I got, the more I mirrored my father. I earned the nicknames "Lee Lizzy" and "Son John G." Both of them I hated and felt like an outcast because I was forced to take on the identity of an invisible man. After all, he had forgotten who I was, yet I was forced to walk in his shadow. I sometimes felt like a social misfit in my own family because everyone always talked about how much "I" looked like him. Too escape, I would zone out into my imaginary space in order to cope with life.

The loss of my innocence

When I thought life couldn't get any worst, it did. I was eight when my innocence was stolen. This first incident occurred shortly after my mother's first onset. We had walked across town to a family member's house because my mom was in the middle of one of her episodes. When we arrived, Mom was very emotional, and everyone's attention was immediately focused on consoling her. We were told to go hang out with the other kids while they cared for my mother. A close friend of their family, who was much older than I was, lured me into a bedroom with candy. I didn't know it was in exchange for my innocence. For a long time I carried guilt, and I blocked out a major chunk of the memory of my childhood. I blocked out the physical pain resurfacing later, but I remember staring at the colorful window curtains in an effort to avoid the unbearable expression on his face as I laid on the floor in fear, with my dress up to my chest, my underwear beside me, and my legs spread. Then, I remember nothing afterwards because I checked out and went to my safe place.

My aunt brought me back into reality with the sound of her scolding for she was very upset with me. I remember her questioning, and then blaming me for going into the room with the older boy. I was called "fast," and was told I had no business being around the older boys. From what I recalled, not much was said to him, and from then on, I was labeled, "fast." That was the last time I remember anyone ever saying a word about it, but I felt ashamed and in trouble. I tried to bury it, and believe whatever bad happened to me was because I was bad, and I somehow deserved it. I became even quieter, withdrawn, and overwhelmed by sadness.

Although I was really young, I thought about running away to find my father because I wanted to be with him. I knew I couldn't find him and I blamed myself for his absence. Maybe he was too ashamed of us, and wasn't ever coming back. I soon learned to bury my hurt. I was confused and scared, and all I had learned was I was supposed to stay away from older boys, and keep them from touching me. I became afraid of men, big boys, and even boys my age. My innocence was forever broken as I was on my way to more victimization and abuse.

Grandma, who had done her best to fill in for my mother, became our pillar. She did a lot for us and tried her best to help fill the void of our mamma and missing daddy. However, she was a strong figure in the church community, and often traveled to various church conventions. About three years after Mom's onset, Grandma became overwhelmed because it was obvious my mom's mental illness caused instability. Despite Grandma's best efforts to keep us together, there came a point where my mom was no longer able to care for us, and we were dispersed among relatives, which was the demise of our family structure. Truth be told, my sisters and I never lived together again as a family.

I was about ten-year-old when I went to live in the same household where I was first sexually molested. It was difficult living there because I couldn't escape the memory of what had been done to me. My aunt never trusted me, assuming my mind was clouded with boys. However, boys were the farthest thing from my mind because I feared them. After living there a couple years, I was sent to live with Grandma when I was twelve. This was a relief, as I was finally away from the emotional chaos haunting me. It was Grandma, me—and the two-year-old brother my mom had conceived during one of her long stays in the hospital. It was summer, and I was settling in with Grandma and my transition into middle school. Inside I felt deeply saddened, but life was once again livable.

We lived in the projects, and I begin to hang out with a group of girls living there. I loved to skate around the neighborhood. One day I asked Grandma if I could roller skate to the store. She said yes, but with hesitation. I was so excited, and I tried to skate as fast as I could so I could prove to her I was responsible enough to go alone, and come right back. Little did I know danger was waiting for me. As I skated down the street, I noticed someone behind me, so I skated faster, hoping to put some distance between us. This was the man who would stare at me from time to time at the park. However, I did not know his name, but I remember kids in the neighborhood teased him. I actually felt sorry for him because I knew how it felt to be picked on and teased.

Now he appeared out of nowhere. At first I wasn't sure he was following me, so I crossed to the other side of the street. He followed. I was scared because I had never spoken to him before, and I did not know why he was after me. I skated and skated, hoping and praying he did not catch up with me. My mind was racing faster than my feet, and I was afraid. I could not skate fast enough, and he caught me. I was shocked because I was now staring fear in the face. He had full control of my fragile body as I tried to wiggle away, but he threw my body against a tree. I could feel the sting penetrate my spine as his hot breath brushed against my neck. I screamed, but he silenced me as he forced his course tongue down my throat. I gagged for breath as I tried to escape. Whenever I showed resistance, he would sling my body back in the position where he wanted it. I soon realized the more I tried to escape, the more aggressive he became. He tore off my shirt and began to fondle my underdeveloped breast. He squeezed and sucked and squeezed and sucked until my entire chest felt depleted. I was silenced by fear.

However, a voice inside of me was trying to find its way out. I prayed and cried inside of my head. "Lord, help me!" Suddenly a loud scream of terror was released. I startled both him and myself because I did not realize I had such power within me. All of a sudden a neighbor peeked out of his door and yelled, "Hey what's going on out here." I was paralyzed as I watched my attacker stumble and then run off. I gathered myself, took off my skates, and ran to the store because my grandma was waiting for my return. I did not see which direction my attacker went, nor did I look back to see if the neighbor had come off his porch. It was hard to contain myself, so I cried and cried as I ran. I ran in the store, got what my grandma needed and hurried home.

The way home was torture. I was afraid he would come back to finish what he had started. In my bare feet, I ran as fast as I could past every bush, alley, and side street. I was very quiet, and I never told a soul as I begin to lose more of myself. Part of me was starting to think it was something I had to take. After all, it had happened before, so I buried it and moved on. Besides, I did not want to get scolded or blamed for it, so I shut my mouth.

I became very afraid of men, not wanting to be around them. As my body began to develop, I became even more terrified and would avoid the interactions with men every way possible. Over the next few months, I would see this guy at the park from time to time. He would stare at me, and I would pretend I did not notice him as I quickly disappeared. I remember wishing my daddy would come and set him straight for what he had done to me.

This Journey Was Not by Choice

At thirteen, I didn't believe in miracles, but my dream of my father returning had come true. There he was, my daddy, the tall, muscular, brown-skinned man I remember. He appeared to have no interest in me. He had come to Grandma's house to speak to her. I was overwhelmed as I stared at him, shocked by how much I resembled him. He didn't look anything like the daddy I had created in my imaginary world, but he was my daddy—and he was here. I was speechless, and I didn't know how to feel. For years, I had longed for him to rescue me, and now he was here. I was confused until he revealed to my grandma he had come to let her know he had taken my two older sisters to live with him. My two older sisters, who were fifteen and sixteen, and were getting into trouble, and he thought he could father them, but he hadn't been a parent in years. I never knew how they found him, but I was happy they did.

Not once did he mention me or take any interest. I felt so abandoned, and envied my sisters because they actually got to be with him. Deep down I was hoping it worked out for them, and once they were settled in, he would come back for me. Because my grandma didn't let me have any contact with my father, I wasn't able to talk to my sisters while they were living with him. They were with my father for a very short time because it wasn't long before he gave up raising them. I'm not sure what happened. Living with Grandma, I was often kept out of the loop. There were rumors my dad couldn't control them as easily as he thought, and he quickly gave up and they eventually returned to my mother's family.

It was then my sisters went to live with my mother's relatives, and any traces of my dad were wiped clear. I also realized my father was never coming back for any of us because he was moving out of state. I was forced to grieve my loss of hope. As I got older, I learned how to cope by concealing my pain behind a mask. However, less than a year later, the memory of my father would resurface. All of a sudden, we were awakened in the middle of the night by a loud beating on the door and bright lights beaming through the windows. I jumped out of bed and followed Grandma down to the front room. I could feel the house vibrate as they continued to pound away. I thought they were going to kick the door in or walk through it.

"Grandma, what do they want?" I asked as I stood behind her as she approached the front door. No one was in the house but Grandma, my little brother, and me.

"Who is it?"

"It's the FBI," responded a loud, manly voice.

"What do you want? Ain't no trouble around here!" Grandma shouted back as she was opening the door.

"We are looking for _____ _____! Do you know where he is?" They were looking for my father. Although we didn't know where he was, we were forced out of the house, and they searched every room. I was confused. How did they know who we were, and why were they looking for my father here? After it was all clear, we entered the house, and the man gave Grandma a piece of paper with a number on it and told her to call if she heard anything from him. Grandma said very little to me as she ordered me back to bed. I was puzzled, and I wanted to know what was going on. It wasn't until months later my oldest sister told me the police were searching for him because my father had killed his wife. She also shared a little about what she witnessed while living in their house. I was in disbelief and did not know how to feel about hearing the news because I had never met her or her children.

Grandma was approaching seventy, and took care of us with her disability check and welfare, so at age fourteen, I got a summer job doing landscape in the projects. The crew consisted of ten youth workers between the ages of fourteen and seventeen, and one adult crew leader. The first thing I noticed—I was the only female. This made me a little uneasy, but I needed the money for school clothes. It did not take long before I became the target of sexual assault and physical abuse. The crew leader would force the boys to kiss, touch, and fondle me. Many of the boys were more than willing, and would be eagerly waiting for their opportunity to sexually exploit me. However, a few hid in the shadows because they knew it was wrong. Those boys who refused were teased and called names because of their lack of participation. I was once again humiliated, and he threatened to kill me and my family if I said anything or stopped coming to work. I had never experienced this kind of fear. I dreaded going to work, but I felt I had no choice.

I learned to mentally escape my surroundings and allowed them to do whatever he requested them to do. I endured this in secret for the entire summer, and was relieved when the job ended. I thought this was another event I would bury, but one day, one of the boys told. I will never forget the day. I was upstairs in my room getting ready for the start of school when suddenly I heard a loud knock on the door. This knock was unfamiliar, yet it reminded me of a previous event when the FBI came. I stood at the top of the stairs as Grandma opened the door. Again it was the police, and this time they were here for me. My grandma glared up at me in an effort to seek a reason for their visit. I was clueless because I couldn't think of anything I had done to warrant their visit. As I approached the front door, I begin to see familiar faces beside the police. There was the head supervisor who had interviewed me, one of the crewmembers who had been reluctant to touch me, and his parents. I made eye contact with my former co-worker, and it all suddenly made sense.

Before I could get close enough to say anything, Grandma threw her large frame in front of my narrow body and kindly said, "Sir, why are you here? We don't want no trouble!" The supervisor explained to my grandma his version of the story gathered from some of the boys who were willing to tell. Then the police requested my attendance in an effort to get my statement, and identify the man who had assaulted me. Grandma stared sternly at me, turned back to the officers, and said strongly, "She don't need to go causing no more trouble. Ain't no harm been done to her. She will be fine." She closed the door and whispered to me, "Some things just need to be left unsaid." From then on, I understood what she meant. I nodded in agreement and hurried off to my room to catch a last glance of the commotion outside.

I again buried my trauma and adjusted my mask. I was beginning to see a pattern with men, and I thought perhaps I was better off without a father. A few months later, I ran into someone who told me my father was dead. This was never confirmed, but no one in the family knew differently, and for the next five years, I believed it.

By the time I was fourteen, I was beginning to realize I needed a daddy to validate me. I wanted him to come rescue me because the tragedies in my life were taking a toll on me. I was depressed, angry, and confused because nothing in my life could validate me. Grandma was an old lady who didn't have a clue as to how to deal with my sorrows, my mother was struggling with her mental illness, and my dad was presumed dead. The thought of suicide haunted me because I was a young girl who needed her father to give her a princess crown. Although I grieved his death, I secretly held onto a small glimmer of hope.

I'm sure my childhood memories have caused you to think about your own childhood tragedies and relationship with your father. In the next chapter, "Daddy, Where Did You Put My Crown?" goes more in depth as it exposes the effects of fatherlessness on very young girls. If you still don't think little girls need their daddies, hold that thought until you read the next three chapters.

CHAPTER 3

Daddy, Where Did You Put My Crown?

Her mother dresses her for her crowning. However, it is her father who places the crown on her head. If her father fails to crown her, she does not learn how to appreciate her value and self-worth. If daddy teaches her she is his princess, she will grow up expecting to be her husband's queen.

"I ain't got no daddy!"

"Ms. Moore, I'm sending this young lady to you now because she cannot be in my class." Ms. Turner protested with authority as she went on to explain her concern on the phone. I tried to visualize the image she struggled to describe as I reluctantly accepted her request. In her voice was a desperate urgency demanding my immediate attention. "I can't believe Ms. Turner. She knows how busy we are," I mumbled to myself as I hung up the phone. This was the beginning of the school year, and counselors were in a race with the clock. Schedules needed to be corrected, classes needed balancing, and new students were coming at a rate of five an hour. I had no time for a student with dress-code issues. However, I waited impatiently for this student to appear before me.

To ease my frustration, I grabbed my bottle of slightly chilled water, and took a sip. As I prepared to swallow, I caught a glance of her image as she entered. Somehow the water had missed its destination, and I choked. The little princess had finally arrived. Underneath the overdone, unperfected makeup was a face as pure as gold. I could see the immaturity of her youth peeking through as she tried to mask it by acting well beyond her youth. However, she could easily be mistaken for a girl barely beyond the gates of elementary school. There stood her thin, fragile, undeveloped body, just barely over four feet tall without the massive phony ponytail planted on the top of her head.

As she struggled to maintain her balance, it was obvious she had not yet entered puberty. However, her wardrobe would tell a different story. She wore a cut-off fitted white denim jacket, and underneath was a sparkly spaghetti strap tank top exposing her invisible cleavage. It also partially revealed her mid-section in an effort to show off her fake, heart-shaped navel piercing that appeared out-of-place. To match, she wore a short, red mini-skirt, barely long enough to contain what was underneath it. To top it all off, she wore a pair of four-inch wedges more appropriate for the feet of someone much older. Although she appeared to be dressed to impress, her attitude spoke a different tune. She was angry, but I smiled gently, welcomed her in, and closed my door.

After introducing myself, I got right to the point and explained to her why she got a VIP (Very Important Person) pass to my office. "Do you know why you are in my office?"

"I guess because I was playin with the boys? We weren't even doin nothin!" she said as she crossed her arms, and expressed her pouting stance. "My teacher is really forcin it! Can I call my momma?" she blurted out without ever taking a breath, obviously on the defense.

"Boy, you sure know how to rock those shoes," I said to her in an effort to connect with her. She cracked a smile and struck a pose as if she was seeking my approval. "Are those your shoes"? I asked.

"Naw, they my momma's."

I was shocked but curious as I continued to engage her in conversation. "Does your mamma know you got on her shoes?"

"Yep, she let me wear em." As my curiosity grew, my questions got bigger. "Does you dad know you're wearing those shoes?"

"I ain't got a daddy!" she blurted out, appearing to show little concern. As we continued, she went on, unknowingly sharing her family dynamics. "I ain't got a daddy; my mamma ain't got a daddy, etc."

I explained she had been sent to my office because Ms. Turner was very concerned with how she was dressed, and how overly friendly she was with the boys. Although this young girl was a few years away from her teens, she admitted she really liked boys and the attention she got from them. She reluctantly agreed, I handed her the phone and instructed her to call her mom. On the other end, I could hear the rise of anger from a young female voice. The call must have woken her up. "What you do now? I'm tryna sleep!" she yelled as her daughter smirked and handed me the phone.

I quickly apologized and explained our school dress code policy. The mother expressed her frustration as I explained in detail how her daughter appeared before me. Before hanging up the phone, she agreed to bring in some more appropriate clothing for her daughter to wear at school. While she anxiously waited for her mother, we continued to talk. I had years of experience talking to older teenage girls about the dress code, etc. However, I didn't understand why a little girl who appeared to be so pure stood before me.

The multigenerational fatherless epidemic

As I inquired, she was very open, and had no problem sharing her story. It was obvious she was from generations of fatherlessness, and was only mimicking the women who surrounded her. Her own mother was fourteen when she became pregnant by an older man, and her mom was also born to a teen mom and absent father. When the mom appeared, she was a mere reflection of her daughter. At first glance, she could have easily been mistaken for one of our students. The attire she modeled was even more revealing than what her daughter wore. After a brief conversation, and the clothing exchange, she was on her way.

This little girl and I continued to have frequent visits, and she later disclosed her mom was a stripper. This girl is likely to repeat this cycle because at least two generations of fatherless women came before her—and the effects are obvious. The reality: as she learns the game, she too may accept this superficial crown that defines her false sense of self-worth. It's disheartening for when society encounters her, she may have already entered into a life of sexual abuse, physical abuse, suicide, teen pregnancy, drug abuse, poor school performance, and criminal activity. She may even be viewed as a criminal, a manipulator, or one of the bad girls.

It's not because she was destined to be bad, it's because she lacked the love and validation she needed from a father. Daddy, where did you put her crown? Better yet, daddy where did you put her self-worth, validation, and love? A little girl needs this crowning from her daddy to validate her self-worth as she journeys through the milestones from childhood into womanhood. The above family dynamic is an example of the multi-generational fatherless epidemic. It is obvious there is a disconnection of the father's role altogether. Without counseling and interventions, this young daughter learns how to mimic her mother as she masters the art of self-exploitation to mask the longing to be loved by her father.

However, it is clear she is already longing for validation because she is seeking the wrong attention from boys her age. Later as the longing to be loved and validated intensifies, she may seek to fill this need in sexually driven relationships with men she subconsciously views as a daddy. If she does, she becomes accustomed to masking the abandonment through the sexual exploitation of her body, and like her mom, the false sense of love and validation will become a financial stability and/or a way of life.

Crowning—validating her self-worth

As you read on in future chapters, you may notice I often reference the word "crowning." My definition of crowning refers to the validation of self-worth that a young girl receives from the relationship she has with her father. When she is crowned by her father, she understands her worth, and knows she has her daddy who will love and protect her. This is usually ignited by the natural bonding experience occurring between a daughter and her father. This bonding teaches her how to gain her own sense of identity as she learns to validate herself as a young lady, woman, wife, mother, and career woman, etc. Without this crowning, she lacks the knowledge needed when making positive choices, protecting herself, and having confidence as she approaches the many milestones through her life.

Although one would assumes this fact is a given, millions of little girls long for their absent daddy's crowning. They are easily forgotten about, because they silently wait in the background, hoping someone, anyone, will reach out and crown them. Such a little girl may not realize she is searching for the love of her absent father as much as she realizes she desires to receive some form of validation from the opposite sex. Many of these girls begin acting out their feelings (longing to be loved by daddy) at a very early age, long before it becomes sexual.

Here is a prime example: a single mother called me at my office inquiring about therapy for her seven-year-old girl who seemed to be overly friendly with men, even when she didn't really know them. The mother reported she had noticed on a few occasions while at church her daughter would seek attention from random men. When she found an opportunity, she would climb up on a man's lap, wrap her arms around his neck, grab his hand, etc. There was a rising concern among other parents because she was also seeking affection from her playmates' fathers. The mother also reported she wasn't aware of any history of sexual abuse, and her daughter wasn't demonstrating any sexual gestures. However, she did admit she had been recently asking about her father, who had been absent since her birth. She had asked her mom why some kids had a daddy—and she didn't.

This mother informed me the dad went to prison when her daughter was a few months old, and she never had a relationship with him then afterwards. Because she wanted a better life for her daughter, she thought it was best to keep her away from her father and his way of life. She never dated because she wanted to focus on raising her daughter. Other adults immediately assumed this little girl was expressing some kind of sexual interest in men. However, in my professional opinion, I believe she was acting out her desire to be daddy's little princess. In fact, it seems she is very aware of his absence, and is beginning to long for him.

If this is overlooked, she will continue to do whatever it takes to gain the attention she desperately needs to obtain her crowning moment. This longing will continue to fester, because it is what she needs to feed her self-esteem, and it is only seen through the eyes of her father. Because of this longing for love, she becomes an open target for sexual abuse, and many predators are aware of her long before society knows who she is. If this little girl grows accustomed to her daddy's absence, the longing intensifies, and as she continues to seek out validation. She becomes vulnerable as she unknowingly increases her risk of exposure to sexual abuse and/or sexual exploitation. Desensitized to the role of her father, she accepts her fatherlessness as being normal.

The affects of social media

The reality of it is, because these little girls don't know what it means to be loved and validated, they search for misinterpretations of it. With the growing trend of social media, these young girls are getting more accustomed to sexually exploiting their own bodies in front of the world. The other day while on Facebook, I was in shock as I saw people commenting on a picture of two partially nude twelve-year-olds, in a bathtub posing in very sexual positions. I couldn't believe the names they were being called. Although the poses seemed really disturbing, I stared at the little faces glowing with innocence. I could see the longing for love speak through their eyes, and I became immediately fixated because I was drawn to their pain. Sadly, it was familiar to me.

Scrolling down, I discovered a video of two preschool girls in bikinis dancing like strippers in a nightclub. I believe they call this dance "twerking." I am still trying to figure out the meaning of it. I have never seen little girls dance in such a sexual way. What was most alarming, it appeared they were being cheered on by their young mothers, barely in their twenties. My heart aches as I scream out, "Where did their daddy put their crowns?" I'm not speaking only of the little ones dancing, but also of the young mothers cheering.

Some girls are using Facebook to fulfill their longing to be loved, others are going to chat rooms, etc. While such a girl may not be comfortable exploiting herself before the world, she may surf the Internet in search of conversation with someone looking to falsely validate her worth. She is unaware of the predators lurking in her shadow, awaiting her arrival. Although she may be just seeking attention, she is sucked into an emotional connection as the predator soothes the longing and desperation left by her absent father. At first he appeals to her by appearing sweet, understanding, and friendly, then he demands more and more of her time as he gauges his leverage. Because she has no idea of what she is into, she is not aware of the danger of him winning her trust. He pretends to love her, protect her, and promises to grant her every wish to get her emotionally locked in.

Once she is locked in, he will then attempt to lower her to him. At this point, she is on the brink of danger, because longing to be loved by daddy will draw her right into his arms. This process can occur over a period of time, and in most cases it may go unnoticed for months. I worked with a couple of preteen girls who were discovered before they were lowered into their predator's arms. In some cases, these little girls were pretending to be grown women, when in reality they were only eleven or twelve. This can be a very traumatic experience that carries lifelong effects, because these men eventually reveal their intent. I have witnessed the emotional trauma girls experience after an encounter with online predators. It is a very scary experience, and the girl is often left feeling violated, afraid, and confused.

Vulnerability in the community

Not only are fatherless girls at risk of encountering online predators, they are an even easier target for the predators who mask themselves as the helpers of our communities. They can be a friendly neighbor, teacher, coach, uncle, mother's boyfriend, etc. This predator is the familiar father figure who secretly engages in inappropriate interactions, which can be mistaken as friendly gestures, but are innocent enough to fulfill the girl's longing to be loved. As the predator builds an emotional connection, he tells her how pretty she is as he lowers her into a friendly, playful relationship. Before he becomes sexual with her, he eases his way in and gets her accustomed to their close encounters. She does not understand his behavior is inappropriate, because she has no knowledge to gauge what a daddy's love looks like.

By the time the abuse has been discovered, she has buried the secret and her perception of her self-worth becomes more distorted as she accepts it as a way of life. If it is never discovered, it is carried as a lifelong secret until she has the courage to tell someone.

Without therapy, she carries the betrayal, guilt and shame, secrets of abuse, feeling of abandonment, and longing to be loved. As a result of her pain, this fatherless little girl begins to engage in risky behaviors in order to find the validation she is longing for. This longing quickly turns into desperation, and she runs out of the gate like a wild horse in any direction.

Because of her immaturity, she lacks the ability to rationally evaluate situations long enough to make a sound judgment. She has now becoming more disconnected from her core feelings, and is not aware of the daddy's love she is really seeking. By the time someone discovers her pain, she has already positioned herself in a role far exceeding her youth, as she becomes a victim to men who are far from deserving her innocence. Because she was hurting long before she arrived at this place, she has already grown accustomed to sacrificing herself to satisfy the innate desire to be loved valued, and protected.

In the next chapter, these fatherless daughters become voices as they share stories of life without the love of their father.

CHAPTER 4:

Letters to Their Fathers

Even if my father never had the courage to read my letter, I have found peace because I was finally able to voice my truth. When I acknowledged my pain and released it, I became free.

Did you ever write a letter to someone because it was to difficult to speak to them in person? If so, you can imagine the pain that was released as these daughters share their story. I have found writing to be a source of healing, and I spent most of my life writing through my pain. This is one of the chapters closest to my heart, because it gives other fatherless daughters the opportunity to speak to their fathers. For many of them, this will be the first they are voicing their secrets and pain. The letters I wrote to my own father helped me to release a lot of the emotional baggage I had carried from childhood. One letter I wrote to my father can be found here in this chapter. However, the full letter to my father can be found in Chapter 8, "Am I Not Your Daughter?"

Perhaps you may be wondering why I think these letters are significant. In my private practice, when I work with girls and women who suffer from self-esteem issues, broken marriages, abusive relationships, etc., I draw a family genogram so I can get an understanding of the family dynamics. A genogram is a diagram outlining the history of the behavior patterns occurring within a family over generations. For example: divorce, death, alcohol and other drug abuse (AODA), suicide, etc. As a part of the intake, I ask a series of in-depth questions about their relationship with their parents, siblings, grandparents, etc. This is where I get the most accurate understanding of how they have come to discover themselves. It's not surprising the majority state their father is/was physically absent, emotionally absent, or both.

Listen to their pain as these courageous daughters share the heartbreaking stories of their survival as they navigated through life without a sense of love and self-worth. Although they are of different races, ages, and beliefs, what brings them together is the pain and abandonment of being fatherless. As you read these stories, you will find some of them never knew their fathers, while others grew up in the same house with him. However, all of them grew up feeling fatherless because none of them grew up feeling loved by their fathers. A father's physical presence has no substance if he is emotionally absent, because his daughter still grows up without him.

Dear Dad,

I hold no anger or bitterness in my heart. I do wish we could have a regular relationship. I really wish it could be the typical father-daughter relationship. But I know that is wishful thinking. I often wonder why you were not a part of my childhood. I often wonder why my sisters and I did not have a male role model in our life. I was told you left when I was born, and as a small child, I really thought it was my fault you were not there. I never said anything to anyone because I did not want anyone to know the secret—that it was because of me, my sisters and I did not have a dad. Sometimes I wished I had never been born and I thought maybe then my Mom, Dad and sisters would have been the perfect family.

I remember wishing and praying that one day you would come and be a part of our lives. I have no recollection of you as a child. I remember hearing someone say you looked like Lionel Richie, and so that was the mental image I had of you. I do remember you coming to visit us when I was seven or eight. I remember meeting my two brothers, but still I could not remember your face from that visit.

I myself had no idea your absence from my life would have such an impact on my life. I cannot say it was all for the bad but there was definitely some negative results. I do think, had you been there I would have been a far more-confident woman. I do blame my low self-esteem on not having my dad telling me how valuable I am, and defining my self-worth to me from an infant to womanhood.

I know I have made a lot of poor choices, but for the most part, I consider myself to have turned out very well.

Forever Yours, Another Statistic, age 39

Dear Daddy,

I want you to know I grew up hating and fearing you

every day of my life. I wished I could have been like all my friends with dads who showed how much they love them. You never spoke it or showed me love. I was told every time you beat me, you were showing me how much you loved me. This taught me if you weren't beating me or degrading me in some way, I wasn't loved. You often told me I'd never amount to anything because I was too stupid. You don't know how much that messed me up.

So many times I badly wanted to hear you say something nice to me, and gave me encouragement and guidance. I felt I was never good enough for anyone to love. I felt so worthless my whole life. All I got was put downs, ridicule, and beatings. You only had negative things to say to me, or looked for a reason to beat me. I needed you to teach me how a man should care for and treat me.

I dropped out of high school and rushed into marriage to get away from you. I ran to the first guy who told me he loved and cared for me. I spent thirty-five years in a marriage where I was constantly mistreated because I had learned I wasn't worth any more than that. Once in my forty-nine years of life, I wish I could have gotten a hug, or you told me you were proud of me. On my wedding day, you said sad and disheartening words while you walked me down the aisle.

I settled with a man just like you. During our entire marriage, he had affairs, and continued to use me until his lover was clear and free. Like you, he emotionally abused me. I never knew how to stand up for myself, or have pride in myself, to know I was worth much more than what he offered. Instead I felt insecure, unworthy, and unloved. All I wanted was for someone to love me, and for all those years, I thought that was all I needed, but it wasn't.

I was still searching, wishing, hoping for my father's love, approval, encouragement, guidance, support, and a hug or two. All these years, I took care of you after Mom passed, when your other children refused. A "thank you" or "I appreciate you" would have been nice. I thought this would have changed how you treated me. I tried so hard to please you, and to get you to love and care about me.

I spent eleven years reliving my childhood as you continued to put me down and ridicule me. Because of this, I tried to take my own life. However, my love for my family saved my life. I wish I could have heard you say you loved me before you passed. I sincerely feel you showed me love and appreciation when you waited for me to come to the hospital to hear me say I loved you before you passed. You didn't speak, but I could tell when you looked at me, your eyes said it all. Everything I waited my whole life to hear: I love you, Thank you, I appreciate you, you are a great mom, I'm proud of you, and anything else a father is expected to say to their daughter. Thank you for waiting for me to come so I could tell you I'd be okay.

Now I am working on being okay and learning to love myself. I know I am worth being loved. I have taught my kids how to love, and to be loved, so their lives would be different. I am now trying to figure out how to start all over after loving and trusting someone I thought loved me for so many years.

With my son and daughter's support, I will survive. Through therapy, I can say I forgive you, Dad, and may you rest in peace.

Love, your daughter M.A.B

Dear Daddy,

You were the first man who was supposed to capture my heart. I wanted so desperately to love my daddy. However, I couldn't because you weren't there. I grew up watching other little girls love and cherish their daddies. All I could do was dream of what it would be like to love you, and you love me back. I felt abandoned and often alone.

I grew up without either of my parents, and I made it this far. I thank God for not allowing me to turn to alcohol or drugs. While during my self-discovery, I realized a part of my healing would come from writing a letter to you, my father. Although some of what I say may be hurtful, I believe you deserve to know the truth about how I have felt over the years.

Before I could begin to address the issues I have had in my relationships with men, I realized I needed to begin at the root. My hope is to obtain healing and an understanding of where I came from in order to understand where I am headed, and to figure out where I need to go. I do hope this healing brings closure. I also hope we can establish a better relationship. I would be lying if I said I did not need you.

Even today, I desire love and acceptance from you. A daughter is never too old to seek the love she desires from her parents. I know I will never have the relationship I desire with my mother because of her illness. However, I do think a better relationship with my father is possible. I am praying God leads us to that.

I can't help but wonder what it was like for you on the day I was born. My mind is flooded with so many questions. Did you fall in love with me? Did you hold me close to his heart? Did you sing to me? What did you say the moment I came into the world? Do you remember what I looked like and smelled like? Are there any significant historical events you can recall happening on that day? I have always been afraid to ask because maybe you wouldn't have any memories. It was safer for me to pretend I meant something to you.

As a mother of six sons, I cherish many special moments from each one of my son's birth, as if it was yesterday. I can remember how much each weighed, how long they were, whether their hair was straight or curly, and even significant historical events happening around us. My oldest son is now twenty, but I still remember the day of the week he was born.

I was barely three years old when you left. I often felt it was not fair I didn't have you there. I hate that I did not get to know who you are. I never knew if you loved me or not. I can't remember much about you. I remember you being gone, and you never came back. From that day on, my heart was forever broken. I was too young to understand how this event would later impact my like. I never got to ask you why? Why did you leave us? Did we not mean enough to you for you to stay? I wanted to know you. I wanted you to protect me from all of the bad things that were about to happen. I wanted you to show me what love was, and what it wasn't. I dreamed of you. I would always imagine you would someday appear like a superhero coming to save the day.

I grew up feeling ashamed because you weren't there. I couldn't tell anyone who you were because I didn't know for myself. I wish I could say I remembered you taking me to the park, or celebrating one of my many birthdays. I can't because you were not there. I often felt like I was no one important because I couldn't even keep my own dad around. Many years my heart ached because I was growing up, and you were missing it all. I wanted to make you proud of me. I wanted you to know I was trying to please you. I needed to know you loved me, and I needed to learn from you. I wanted to know how it felt to be held in your arms. I don't remember.

Your daughter in pain, SM, age 42

Dear Dad,

Most of the time, family life wasn't bad. I love you, and you know I was daddy's girl. However, my personal security disappeared when I was four years old. Mom and you had a big fight. I didn't know then it was because you had gone out and was drunk. All I remember was sitting in the big overstuffed chair and watching Mom. She told you, "No more" and walked out the door. My brother and I watched her go from the window, and began yelling and screaming, "Mommy, come back. Mommy, come back!" You tried to make it all better, but we both knew you were the one who "made" her go. The next morning, we woke up to find her back and making breakfast, but I never forgot that day.

When our family relocated to Minnesota, the worst of the drinking began. You became friends with people at our church, one of whom was into making wine in his basement. Often, Mom and we kids would go along. After the "sampling" was finished, you would pile us all in the car and drive home intoxicated. One several occasions, you vomited on me as I sat beside you. Family members would excuse you for it, "Oh, poor James, he's so sick. He can't help it." I don't think they realized I knew very well why you were sick. Over time, I developed the mindset you didn't care about me, or you wouldn't drink and vomit on me. Only by God's mercy were we spared a car accident.

You would miss supper and would show up at home drunk when Mom was getting us ready for bed. Usually, you'd lay on the couch, half awake. When I walk past you, you'd holler out, "Elsie! (Your sister's name) It's time to milk cows!" or "Daddy needs a kiss, come give daddy a kiss!" I fell for the second line only once. When I'd get close to you; you'd grab me, give me a slobbery kiss on the mouth, and hold on tight, in spite of my struggling. You wouldn't let go; you kept kissing me. I got really good at watching your eyes. Sober eyes were normal looking, as drunken eyes had red rims, and really drunk eyes were glassy and red rimmed. Glassy eyes meant Dad would get "kissy faced."

If I told you to stop, you would pout and say, "Don't you love your daddy?" The worst part was you didn't remember any of it when you were sober. As a result, I grew up to hate kissing. You were a good dad, when sober. You would do experiments with science, play with us, go on picnics, and take vacations to see our family in Montana. I loved those vacations because you didn't drink when we were on them. I think that is why when you drank, and it hit me so hard. You didn't know my name, and always called by your sister's name.

On my sixteenth birthday, after drinking, you turned to me, and said, "So you're sixteen. You know what they say, "Sweet sixteen and never been kissed or sweet sixteen and never been missed." I missed your telltale glassy eyes with the company there, and before I knew it, I was on the lawn with you straddling me and kissing my face all over.

I think one of the most profound results of your drinking was my not being able to trust people. It took my husband asking me, "Are you ever going to trust me," for me to realize I had a problem. I would get angry and rationalize the anger away, just to keep the peace. I would feel hurt, but be afraid to say anything. As I look back, much of my life was lived in fear of what would happen if I said anything. In spite of your drinking, you are a forgiven Christian man. One memory I have is of you sitting at your desk with your open Bible. God forgives.

Signed Micki, age 49

Dear unknown Daddy,

Through all the pain and the suffering I went through, from birth to being 21 years old, I always wonder who my real father was, and why I haven't met you. My mother never spoke much about you. All she ever told me was I looked like you with hair, and I was always mean like you. When my sisters and brothers came along, I would cry, get mad, and fight them because they had their father in their life. Sometimes they would laugh and tease me saying, "Ha! Ha!." "Your father not around, and our daddy got money." Because he wasn't my father, he treated me like an outsider, like I wasn't even there.

This made me really mad and angry to the point where I'd shut down and not talk to nobody. My mother would always wonder why I was so angry at her and everyone else. It was because I wanted to see you, and until this day, I wonder who you are, and where you are. I will tell you one thing: I hate you! How does a man who knows he has a child not come around? You can't say you don't know about me because we had a DNA test done when I was ten.

Why do little girls have to grow up without a father? What do they do when they meet a man? I wanted to ask you how do I tell a man no, or what type of men to date, and how do you know if they are liars and cheaters? These are some of the questions I needed to ask you. I will never know what you would've told me because I have already been through a lot or things. The guy I had called my stepfather was never a real father. I gave him the right to be called father, but he was a no-good father. He would always argue with my mom because she would let us do things, and he would be like: I wouldn't let them do nothing I would let them sit in the house.

That's why we never respected him. When he died, I was happy because his children were now fatherless like me. Now they can't talk about me not having my father when they don't. I'm a - person and really don't care about nobody but myself. People tell me it's because I didn't have a father figure. I have been hurt physically, mentally, and emotionally by men and other people I don't know. I am only 21, but I have had three daughters. I was 15 when I had my first daughter by a 27-year-old man. I was six months pregnant when she died June 9, 2007 after I gave birth to her. It was because I had been smoking, drinking, and popping pills. At that time in my life, I really didn't care, and wanted to die because all the pain I have been through. I currently have two little daughters. One is three, born in April 2010, a few days before my 18th birthday. Her father is 34, and he is a deadbeat father. My last daughter she is two, born on May of 2011. Her father is also 34.

So unknown father, I have been through it all. I have stayed in shelters, lived from house to house, and have had no help from you or my mom. I hated you while I was little, and I hate you still today. If I was to meet you, maybe I would ease up on the way I feel. You might be able to see you grandchildren one day. You haven't seen them since they were born. As a matter of fact, you haven't even seen me born, and that's a shame. I wonder do you every think of me, ever wanted to meet me, or ever looked for me. I have never met your side of the family. People ask me if I know the Andersons, and I say no because I can't lie. I wish I did because I want my kids know my side of the family.

Sincerely, Your unknown daughter, age 21

Dear Dad,

Growing up without a father took a toll on my life. You left my mother when I was around the age of three. I always wondered what I did for you to walk out on my life, and never return. For me, having to grow up with a single mother was hard. I had seven siblings she had to take care of all by herself. Maybe if I had you there for me, it would have been one less stressor on her. However, since you have been a non-factor, you really never existed in my life.

It's not a day the goes by I don't wish you were here to show me love and affection like a father is supposed to do. You were never around to show me all the things a father teaches his daughter, and this still hurts me to this day. I am now eighteen, and you have a one-year-old granddaughter you have never met. How can you be a dad and abandon your own seed? Now it's up to me to explain to my daughter why her grandfather was never around. When she gets up in age, she will want to know who you are. It hurts to grow up fatherless because I have always wanted and needed a father figure in my life. I am always wondering if and when you will come searching for me.

Signed Brittany, age 18

Dear Daddy,

For years I wanted to tell you how your presence was missed in my life while I was growing up. You provided money, and would see me here and there, but I still longed for your full-time presence. There were times I wouldn't see you for months, and I think that the longest time was about a year. When I did finally see you, I didn't feel like your baby girl. However, in my mind I hoped it was just my thoughts.

As a child I was hurt from my environment and would wish I could be with you. In my mind, you could do no wrong as I would believe every word you said. However, as I became of age, I started to realize I wasn't a major priority in your life. I started hating you, but it was when God revealed to me the ugliness in my heart that I knew it wasn't right. I had to repent and from that day forward, I wanted a relationship with you. The relationship we have now is better, but sometimes I see you as just another person, instead of a father.

What really upsets me you never have apologized for not being there, and you continue to make excuses. A child doesn't understand the excuses when they are young. However, as a young lady, I should have had my dad there to teach me and give me the love I deserved.

It's all in the past now, but I needed to tell you the truth about what's in my heart. Even to this day, you make promises and don't always keep them. When that happens, I find myself going back to my childhood, remembering the promises that were never kept. I remember a few weeks ago, we almost talked about the past, but I realized you couldn't handle the conversation. I also couldn't control my anger. Dad at times, I'm not even sure if I'm your daughter because the woman I've become is by the grace of God. It was only by his grace I beat the odds that were against me.

Dad, this letter is not meant to hurt you. It's is to help us have a better relationship. I know you are getting older, and you are trying. I want to enjoy these years with you. That is why I want you to know what's in my heart, and where my heart is at. Now I am ready to let all this pain go.

I love you and thank God for you.

CLS, age 24

Dear Father,

I know you are gone now, and maybe I should let go of the disappointments this letter was written two years ago. I can't let go of the pain you caused me, the tears you caused me, and the years you missed. It's so messed up how I can't even remember your face. Did you ever even think of me or even love me? I'm holding onto the pain of your emptiness and never knowing I had a father. You never held me, hugged me, or helped me when I fell. I'm sad you are now gone. I wish I knew you so I could have stopped all of the pain I went through in my childhood. Why didn't you love me?

I wish you could see how much I've grown up. I'm still learning from my mistakes. I have a one-year-old daughter, and I am staying in a shelter now. I'm going to be moving in my own apartment in a few weeks, and I will be graduating from high school in June. Are you proud of me? I met your mother, and I love her. I just feel she treats me different because you are not here, and she doesn't know if I'm really yours.

Signed, Anonymous, age 18

Dear Daddy,

I love you very much. Thank you for staying in my life for so long, and for making me wear things that are appropriate for my age. Sometimes you did some things that were wrong, and it hurt our family. I always try to listen and obey you like a daddy's princess should.

People say I am too smart for my age. I think it is because I want to spread the word of my rough childhood so I can help other kids. Daddy, my life has been a highway with many twist and turns. My heart is broken at the fact you are gone. I learned by your love the years you have been there. It's been some months since you have moved out, but I am still sad. I know I get to visit you often, but it is not the same anymore. I have my good days and bad days. I wish they were all good.

Thank God for Mommy because she is now playing both parents. She loves me, and is kind to me like all mommies are. I forgive you and thank you for still being my daddy, even though you live in a different house now.

Love, Macey age 9

---　✳✳✳　---

Dear Daddy,

I'm afraid of you because you made everybody think I was a fool.

I don't want to date any men. Because of you, I think they are all cruel.

You hurt me in such a way I don't even want to say.

But being touched by my daddy makes me feel a certain way.

I feel alone in a dark room, hoping that God will take this pain away soon.

When I see your face, my hearts just drops and goes boom, boom, boom!

I forgive you for what you did because I know God has taken on your sin.

I know that God is on my side, and you will face him with your lies, and I WIN.

JB, age 18

---　✳✳✳　---

Dear Dad,

   I remember when I was your little princess. You would come home and hold me in your arms and swing me around. You adored me and would take me everywhere you went as I was your best buddy. You kept me from all the harm, and I felt safe and secure in my daddy. Where did those days go? I miss you. So much time has passed, and you didn't bother to check on the well-being of your "baby girl," as you used to say. You said I would always be your baby girl, no matter how many you have after me. Well, you had quite a few, and you forgot all about me, and moved on with your life as if I never existed.

   Daddy why did you leave me? I often cried not knowing why I was haunted by the scary faces, which left me no peace. It was your mistress who could not live with the fact that because of my birth, you made up your mind to stay with your wife. When you went back to her, you never looked back. Do you know how much my life changed after that? The year you left, I was molested by a nineteen-year-old man and his eighteen-year-old sister. They had their way with me, and I was only 5 years old. Then it was your brother who was next in line, and he kept coming back again and again. I was stripped of my innocence, and I begin to feel that this was the thing to do. Daddy Why? Why?

When you came to visit once a year, it was never enough time to tell you what I had endured. By the time I was 10, I had been exposed to sexual, physical, and mental abuse by multiply abusers. I learned to keep it all inside, and to feel safe, I would go back to the days of you holding me in your arms. At 15, I was molested by my stepdad's best friend, became pregnant by him, and married him. Daddy where were you? With all of that abuse, I have learned to hide my pain, and to become an enabler for men who abused me.

I am now 41-years-old now, and I have had two marriages, two beautiful daughters, and three handsome sons. I now know how important it is for a daughter to be esteemed, secure, and loved by her father. With all that I have been through, I still view you as the man I knew when I was younger. I still try to convince myself my daddy loves me. It wasn't until I came to know God this was a reality. He was with every step of the way, and helped me find my self-worth.

Daddy, I have to let go of the pain caused by your absence. I free you from the prison of my bitterness, and I forgive you. I thank God he has never given up on me, and for keeping my mind at peace even in the midst of the storms.

Love Always, Your baby girl, age 41

Dear Papi,

There is so much that has built up on my heart to say to you, and I often ask myself if I were giving the opportunity to talk to you one last time, would I actually be able to say everything I need to get off my chest. The truth is, I feel like my relationship with you was short-lived, and that I feel was not fair to me.

I understand you and my mother had your reasons for going your separate ways, but did that mean you had to stay away from me, too? I feel like you didn't love me enough ... was it so hard for you to come visit from time to time, for heaven's sake, you waited until I was 12-years-old to even try and establish a relationship with me. You missed the most precious moments of my childhood, and then you expected me to welcome you back in my life with open arms. Why would you do me, your only daughter, like that. Was I not enough, did I not deserve your love, after all, I did not ask to be here. I have many aunts and uncles I never built relationships with all because you did not have a relationship with me; this has affected me greater than you could ever understand.

By the time I could actually say I loved you, your days had become limited. Cancer was beginning to take over, and I didn't get to ask all of my questions because I was too worried about your health to think of anything else. I feel like I didn't have enough time to get to know you as a person, and that means I really don't know myself either because I am, after all, a part of you. When you died, I felt like a part of me died as well and anger filled my heart. All I ever wanted was to have MY father be my father. I wanted you to be able to give me away when I got married and spend time with your grandchildren; I wanted to be able to get advice from you when I had to deal with problem areas in my life, but none of that ever got to happen.

Do you realize I really got to have you in my life on good terms for only four years? Even during that time, you had to miss out on things because you were too ill to travel. My heart hurts so badly because of the lack of a relationship I had to have with you, I am not sure if the pain will ever completely go away. Although I know life goes on, I feel as though a part of me will always be missing simply because I never got to know you the way a daughter should know her father.

Sincerely, Your Lost Daughter, age 35

❖❖❖

Dear Dad,

I can never bring myself to say it—the emotion I feel when I look at you. It's been there for as long as I can remember. I never looked at you and thought happy, sweet thoughts. I never looked at you and saw the man I look up to. I never looked at you and felt grateful you were my father. I watched my friends with their dads, and knew that I was different. I never knew, though, just how different I was until I grew up and became the woman I am today.

My brothers and sisters each could write a letter to you and say the same things. They could say how you have scarred them in different ways. They could say how most things in life would be better if you weren't there. They could all say they are disgusted with the way you treat our mother. Some of them have written letters, made phone calls, or tried to sit down with you and have the familiar conversation. One by one, we have come to know you will never change. It was a difficult discovery for all of us, but a discovery we each have made on our own terms.

The memories of my childhood are happy, because my brain has worked hard to block you out. Sometimes, though, I remember the things you did. I remember because I can't help but be scared that my new husband will be anything like you. Terrified to think that part of you will live on in my brothers. Horrified to find that I, myself, have you in me. How did I let this happen? How did everything I hated about you end up in me? How have I become a statistic? I am supposed to be the exception. My future was supposed to be different. I was supposed to rise above all you've done.

The discussion drives me mad. Why do we waste our breath trying to "get to the bottom of this"? There is no conclusion, no answer, and no happy ending. You are my father. You are my worst enemy. You are the reason for the vast majority of my pain. You are all these things, but one thing you will never be is my excuse.

I thank God every day that He is my real father, and that He has provided me with a fairytale. He looks past my insecurities and flaws, and loves me unconditionally. He makes me feel like the most beautiful girl in the world. You will never be able to take that away from me. He is all I need. One day I will have the peace of knowing you are not my father. You have the title, you have the same blood in your veins, but you will never be my father. I have a much better choice that is everything that you are not. So I choose Him, never you.

Your angry daughter LPJ, age 32

Dear Daddy,

I just want you to know that writing this letter was really hard. I really miss you, and it is hard to except that you live in a different state. Some of the girls at my school get to have their dads pick them up from school, and are actually able to hug and kiss them. I watch how they show love to each other, and it makes me sad because I wish I had that with you. I cried one night at my friend's house because she had her whole family there with her. She was born with a daddy in her house.

I love it when I get to come and visit with you, but I hate I only get to see you once a year. I wish I could see you more. I am also sad because of your problems with the police. Daddy, I want you to stay out of trouble. I know you love me, and I am happy for my little sister because she gets to be with you all of the time.

Love Lauren, age 10

HE WHO FIRST HELD HER HEART

---***---

Dear Mr. Dad,

Sometimes I find myself hating you. You have no idea who I am because you don't spend any time with me or talk to me. Most of the time you don't even notice me unless you are yelling at me about something. You always say kids should be seen and not heard, but I don't think that's fair. You think you know me, but I'm not the bad girl you think I am. I'm actually a good girl who wants her daddy to be proud of her good grades. You don't know anything about that because you are always so busy, working, sleeping, or doing stuff for others on your days off. You don't have time for your family anymore.

Sometimes several days go by without you saying anything, and then the first words out of your mouth are, "Why did you do this or that." I don't know why you always accusing me of things I didn't do. I wish you would just talk to me instead of yelling all of the time. You say you don't trust me, then why don't you get to know me?

I know you think you are trying to protect me, but I wish you would let me grow up. I am almost 16, and you still make me go to bed at 9 p.m., and won't let me wear the things I want to wear. I am not trying to disrespect you; I just want to be a teenager. I wish I could talk to you about things like boys, but you won't let me like boys, instead you try to keep me locked up. I think I am old enough to like boys, but I am afraid to tell you that.

I often feel really sad. I wish you would just listen to me because I feel invisible. My friends are able to talk to their dads, but I can't talk to you. I wish you would try to be more like Mom. I can talk to her when you are not around, but she is afraid to stand up to you.

I really want you to know I do have morals, and I do want to make you proud of me. I wish you would see I am a good kid, and I try to make the best decision, even when I make mistakes. I wish thing were like they used to be when I was little. Why did you stop saying "I love you" to me?

Your invisible daughter TVJ, age 19

Dear Daddy, Why Not Me?
Dear Daddy Why Not Me? Why Not Me?
When you looked at me, what did you see?
Not your daughter, one of the three
Three that I knew, but at your funeral
I would learn there were several.
Why Not Me?
Was it because I was dark, round and small,
And your other daughters were light and tall like your wife?
Who gave them life, and not like mine
Who you only saw in your spare time
Time enough to make me, and long enough to hate me?
Why Not Me?
Was I reminder of the affair you had
Outside of your marriage bed?
Somehow, I am not to blame
For being the child who looks so much like you,
But in court you lied and did not claim.
"Not mine." was what you said,
And at that time, I vowed in my heart you were dead.
Why Not Me?
Because you were never a man, but a coward
Afraid to stand up and look forward,
You looked from behind and drowned your sorrows in a bottle.
Not sure what your beverage of choice was,
Just know it took the life you could have lived at full throttle.
Why Not Me?
How I wish I would have asked

HE WHO FIRST HELD HER HEART

Before your breath was your last.
I have a hunch
It has nothing to do with money and such
But rather to do with you not being a true man
That could love me and make me smile instead of frown.
In the hearts of other men. I run in search of the love you turned down.
Why Not Me? I, too, deserve a crown.
JEG, age 45

A daughter's tribute
Dear Dad,

I have been blessed by God with amazing parents. We all have a special relationship and appreciation for both of our parents, but I am a "Daddy's girl," and my other two sisters would probably say the same about themselves. Edward Colbert, Sr. is the epitome of a wonderful father. He was the man of our house. He was also a hair-combing, food-preparing, house-cleaning father. He was a completely hands-on Dad. He bought and brought home the bacon and would fry it up also.

When we were kids, Dad would swim with us and run with us; he was our first example showing us the importance of being physically fit, and he is yet an avid exerciser. He joined the Air Force after high school and spent four years in the service and traveled the world. He and Mom raised us to have a great work ethic and told us we could be anything we desired, even President of the United States of America. To hear this back in the 1960s and 1970s framed our world for amazing hope, opportunities, and success. We tell our girls the same thing to this day.

As a little girl and teen, I loved our weekend evening talks. I just loved to listen to Dad share his life experience, all of those wonderful stories of travel, and his love for learning. I listened to his exciting stories over the years, which framed my desire to follow in his adventurous path as I also later joined the Air Force, and also lived in Japan, just like Dad.

While growing up in their early years, Mom and Dad lived in an overtly racist world. I marvel how they could encourage us to live in a colorblind world. Dad would say to love irrelevant of color, even if they were "green." We also share that with our girls today.

My heart goes out to the millions of girls who didn't have the opportunity to have a father who is a great parent like Dad. He showed me by loving us that we are loveable and worthy of being respected and valued. When I was a little girl, I always said I wanted to marry a man like Dad. Dad and Mom showed us what great parenting looks like, and showed us that much time and prayer is required to positively impact children's lives and future. Dad and Mom illustrated the importance of regular family dinners, daily conversation to catch up on what was going on in our lives, and we learned the value about following current events and sharing different perspectives on them.

We also got to observe my parents' influence as a married couple, and the importance of being committed, respectful and loving, God answered my prayers I asked as a little girl: He blessed me to marry a wonderful man like Dad, Troy who is also a great life partner, fantastic father to our daughters and of course, Dad-approved.

Felicia Robertson, MD

PART II:

Loving with Broken Heart

Chapter 5:
Desperately in Search of . . .

Chapter 6:
A Woman without a Crown.

Chapter 7:
Not in Search of a King.

Chapter 8:
Am I Not Your Daughter?

In this section, I will share more of my personal journey as I transition into adult, and become a heartbroken woman desperately in search of her father's love. When I could not receive his love, as I tried to seek it out as I navigated through life. This section also addresses the warning signs of domestic violence, and when to get help. It closes with a letter to my father, and the beginning of my road to healing and forgiveness.

CHAPTER 5:

Desperately in Search of . . .

Desperation

I feel like I'm afraid of death,
yet I desperately want to die.

My life is filled with too much emptiness,
and inside my soul I cry.

Daddy left me with unfilled holes,
and wondering if he understands.

That my life has been a lonely ship,
and I walk with pieces of my heart in my hand.

As a child it was ripped out, broken,
abandoned, and abused.

Too many pieces to be repaired,
and I don't know if it can be reused.

There is no more need for me to explain,
and no more need to cry.

My heart has been longing for you,
and without you my heart will die.

As a fatherless teenager, I secretly carried feelings of depression, desperation, shame, and emptiness. Although my grandma was a good role model, my relationship with her had become strained because she could not understand my deep sadness. She was doing a good job showing me how to be a holy woman of God. However, we begin to clash because she was not able to help me validate who I was. What she didn't understand was she had unknowingly caused more damage to me by not understanding I needed to deal with the trauma I had experienced. Because I couldn't talk about it, I buried it in my poetry, and pretended to be the perfect honor roll student, when in reality, nothing really mattered as I struggled to mask my pain. On the inside I was hollow, but I managed to pull it together enough to excel in high school. I had battles in my soul because I was searching for something, but I didn't know how to explain to my dear grandma what that something was.

To temporarily satisfy my desperation, I got involved in as many after-school activities just so I could have someone or something validate my worth. I also found comfort in my childhood best friend, Vanessa, and her parents, who accepted me as their own and were very good to me. However, no amount of love could chase away my demons. I tried hard to mask my depression, and pretended that I was an upper middle-class student who came from a two-parent house anywhere except in the projects. During my first two years, I learned how to sculpt my mask and mold into the images of my surroundings by creating a pretend mother and father so people assumed I was one of them. Although I was faking it, life on the outside appeared to be all good. However, one day my life could no longer contain my secrets, and I literally went insane.

It was during my eleventh grade year when I was playing around with a male student. I honestly believe his intentions were not to bring harm to me. However, I couldn't take back what had happened. After our horseplay, I went to sit down on the bay of the window when somehow his finger penetrated me through my clothes. I don't know exactly how it happened because I had my back to him. On that day, I had a moment of insanity and totally lost it. I ran up and down the hallway yelling and screaming, "He hurt me!"

I wouldn't let anyone get near me, not even the staff. I ran from any and everyone because I just needed to escape. All of the emotions from my past poured out, and I became suicidal because I didn't know how to process this event. This was the beginning of my battle with severe depression as I struggled to recapture my make-believe life. After that day, my pain was exposed, and the mask of a perfect student would no longer fit.

My period of desperation

My depression came like a hurricane, and I grew angry and distant from everyone, especially my grandma because I couldn't contain the desperation as I longed for my father. At this point, I was older and determined to seek him out because I desperately needed to find something to which I could attach. As a result, I found my father's parents, and a year later, was introduced to my Uncle John and his wife. Although he was several years older than my father, he was a mirror image of what I remembered of my father. After a brief introduction and several short visits, I was invited to come live with them for the last few months of my senior year. Grandma was very upset, and she was against me reaching out to my father's family because of what my mom had gone through. However, I broke through her protective barrier because this seemed like a good opportunity for me to reinvent my mask. They were upper middle-class, appeared to be searching for what little I had to offer, and were at the ripe age to welcome me as their daughter. I thought I was finally going to get the father's love I had longed for forever.

The relationship with my aunt got off to a smooth start, and although she was the best surrogate mom, I was in search of a bond that connected me with my father. My father was absent, so in my mind, the next best thing was his brother. However, the relationship with my uncle felt difficult and strained. I wanted to reach out to him, but I did not know how, and I was often paralyzed by fear when I saw opportunities to engage with him. The familiar awkwardness filled the room as we sat for hours in silence, attempting to watch a movie. I wanted to feel protected and loved by him, but I didn't understand what I needed to do to connect with him. I secretly longed for him to reach out to me, but he never did. I now had the physically present father I wanted, but he was emotionally disconnected.

After three months of residing with them, I was off to college. I had a full scholarship, and wanted to please my new parents. Things weren't perfect, but I was proud when we arrived at college for orientation day. During the ride there, I felt as if our relationship had made a little progress, and for once I had a father figure who was proud of me. My uncle and I connected as we engaged in various small conversations about my future. This was the first time I felt a connection to him in the three months I lived with them.

About a week after I was dropped off, I received a letter from Uncle John. I remember being overwhelmed with excitement when I pulled the letter out of my mailbox because I couldn't imagine what he had to say. Perhaps he wanted to say he enjoyed the college visit, or maybe he missed me, or even that they might be up for a visit. However, his letter brought me back to the period of depression I had recently put behind me.

"Dear Sonja, Please do not contact me or my wife again. All of my children are now adults, and it is not my responsibility to take on the role of your father."

I was in shock as I read the letter, because I had not anticipated our relationship ending this way. I felt like I had been dropped into a dark hole as my heart raced in fury while tears of sadness filled my eyes. At that moment, I was frozen in time.

Hours passed as I lay buried underneath my blanket, disconnected from everything around me while I struggled to make sense of what had happened. I replayed every moment of our interactions during the few months I had stayed at their house. Nothing! I couldn't think of any significant event that would lead up to this letter. The sound of his voice echoed in my ears as I recited his letter in my head. This was the only father figure I had since my own father. However, he had abandoned me in the most brutal way. I had traded the security of my grandma's love for him—and now

I was left with nothing.

While other girls were excited about their independence, I secretly longed for an opportunity to give up mine. While forced to accept the role as an adult, I became my own guardian, and unwillingly transitioned into adulthood. As a result, I was preoccupied with the idea of suicide—until I made my first attempt as I secretly grieved the loss of my family, my father, and my childhood. Fearful of getting lost in my depression, I reached out for help and was introduced to Mr. J, an African-American male who was assigned as a student liaison for minority students. He seemed to be approaching his forties and appeared very friendly as he overextended himself to me before I had the opportunity to become familiar with him. I found myself pouring out my sorrows as he emotionally embraced me. As time went on, he gradually won my trust, and life seemed doable. In my eyes, he became the father I secretly longed for as he made himself available and attended to my emotional needs.

Although he wasn't married, he had two young children. In exchange for his kindness, I babysat for him on the weekends when his children were visiting. He never paid me for babysitting, but would periodically ask if I needed money or anything. I took it as a simple father-daughter exchange, and after a few months of this interaction, my heart framed that relationship. I begin to feel secure, as he was satisfying my emotional need to be validated and loved by my father. I learned to trust him and spent more time with him.

One Saturday afternoon he invited me to his house to hang out with his kids. Before I could make sense of what was happening, he grabbed me tightly, drew my body close to him, and forced his tongue in my mouth. At that moment, I felt the need to escape. While I desperately tried to get away, he acted as if we were engaged in a playful game as he chased me around the couch. He laughed as he reached at me, trying to grab inappropriate body parts. I said nothing as I picked up speed, gathered distance between us, and made my exit. Once I was through the front door, I felt relief as the chill of my tears touched my cheeks. Again I felt abandoned as guilt overloaded my thoughts. I blamed myself, was once again battling depression, and I made my second suicide attempt. That night I didn't think I could deal with my grief, so I took a bottle of pain relievers and buried myself under my blanket and waited to die. In the process, I must have told one of my friends what I had done, because I woke up in the hospital with tubes down my throat.

After a short hospital stay, I accepted I was now eighteen, and never allowed myself to openly long for that daddy's love. In fact, I buried those feelings altogether, and I recreated a mask by appearing happy, extremely smart, and willing to please. However, inside I had little self-worth, and allowed people to bully me—*and my voice became silent*. My biggest fears were isolation and abandonment. However, I became I became more disconnected from my family. I assumed if I established a secure economic status, it would fix everything. Again, I pretended I came from a good home, had a good relationship with my parents, and had it together. I aspired to be like the people around me, and I realized my career goals could lead me there.

In search of my validation

I was desperately in search of validation, as my addiction to success became a temporary soother. I buried myself in my education, taking the maximum course load without ever earning less than a B. However, all the success in the world never mended my broken heart. I perfected my image as I mimicked my environment and blended into my professional world. On the outside, I became one of them, settled in my books, became comfortable with what I appeared to be, and pretended to have found myself. I created a character where no one knew my shame, and I continued to use my educational cover-up to move along through life. I no longer waited for an opportunity to be daddy's little girl, and the validation I sought from my father was temporarily contained by the desire to succeed. I figured out how to become an adult, and gave myself a superficial crown that validated me as a good woman, high achiever, and a people pleaser. As I struggled with my shame and lack of self-worth, I fine-tuned my mask, to assure a perfect fit. I developed a hard shell on the outside, but on the inside, it was easily broken, and I soon learned to become numb and emotionless until I found myself becoming a victim again.

After two years away in college, I transferred to a local college and reconnected with my father's parents but I never reconnected with my uncle and his wife. My grandparents told me they finally heard from my father and he was in police custody. Before he was arrested and sent to prison for murder, he was living in another state under a different name. I buried my feelings and immediately made myself available to his need for emotional support. I became his communication to the outside world for his entire prison sentence. For years, I kept him in the loop, sent pictures of all of his children and grandchildren, and often wrote words of encouragements. It was obvious our roles were reversed.

I secretly contained my anger as I became an emotional caregiver to the man who had left me heartbroken. I had so many questions that I needed answered, but I buried them and waited for my opportunity to be loved by my father. He promised when he got out of prison, he would come back and make everything right with us. Although I was now nineteen, I was hopeful and anticipated the day when I could be my daddy's little princess. I waited for several years for my father as I continued into womanhood feeling ashamed, confused, abandoned, and unworthy. Although it was obvious I was affected by my father's absence, I am compelled to share another woman's story whose outcome was very different. As you read Josie's story, see if you can uncover the connection between the two of us.

Case study: Josie was raised in an upper middle-class neighborhood, and both of her parents had very successful professional careers. She was never really close to her father because he spent most her childhood working long hours, and at times wouldn't get home until after she had gone to bed. When she was nine, her father moved out, and her parents were divorced a few years later. After the divorce, her relationship with her father grew even more strained. Her parents shared joint custody and joint placement, and she spent equal time with both.

However, she continued to have a difficult time connecting with her father, and their father-daughter bond was never developed. While at his house, there was little interaction between them, and he allowed other things to come in between them. He worked long hours trying to build his business, leaving her alone without any supervision. As a young girl, she would try to reach out to him, but felt he was too preoccupied with his business and personal life. Although she often felt lonely while at her dad's house, as she approached her teens, she preferred being there because she found her way into activities well beyond her youth. When her father left her at home alone, she would wait until he went off to work and leave shortly after he did. She would then enjoy her night out on the town, doing whatever she pleased, but would make sure that she was home before her father returned.

Because her parents did not communicate, her mom had no idea how much freedom Josie had. At her mom's house, she lived an overly structured life that constricted her freedom. She grew more accustomed to her freedom, and often felt frustrated and angry toward her mom. As Josie got older, she secretly resented her father because she felt he was ignoring the significant milestones in her life. She became desperate for attention, and started to get in trouble at school, hanging with the wrong group of girls, and dressing inappropriately for her age.

When at her mom's, she begin to lash out and retaliate against her new stepfather because she didn't want him to replace her father, but secretly envied the relationship he tried to offer her. The more her mom and stepdad tried to maintain structure, the more she resisted. By the time she reached ninth grade, she was drinking, smoking pot, and had various sex partners with boys several years older. When her father finally realized she was out of control, he tried to replicate the structure her mom had in place. She rebelled and became even more angry and defiant.

At fourteen, she became pregnant, but wasn't sure who was the baby's father. Her parents arranged for her to give her baby daughter to a family member, believing it was the best option. She then relocated with her father to another state because there were better opportunities to develop his business. It didn't take long for their family dynamics to return to the norm. Her father started working long hours again, and she connected with a group of girls who reminded her of her past. With her dad's long work hours, and her mom out of state, it was easy for her to be exposed to after-hour activities. When barely sixteen, she met who she thought was the love of her life, and was introduced to the life of stripping. Because of her vulnerability, she had settled into a "love" relationship with a grown man old enough to be her father. She would tell her father she was spending the night at a friend's, while she danced and sometimes performed sexual acts. Instead of living the life as a sixteen year old girl should, she had more sexual experiences than a woman in her thirties.

At seventeen, she ran away from home and was sexually exploited by the man who convinced her he was the only one who loved her. By the time she turned eighteen, she was totally inducted into prostitution, and was forced to travel from state to state. However, she hated it, but would be severely beaten when she refused to do what this man commanded. She accepted this way of life, and became heavily involved in drugs and alcohol to wash away the deception. After over fifteen years of being his captive, she eventually escaped the life of prostitution, but found herself victimized by one abuser after the other.

Now a woman in her early forties, she sits across from me in a therapy session as she struggles to find her identity and self-worth. What is ironic is the fact that this woman and I are exactly the same age, our stories are very different, yet we both grew up affected by fatherlessness.

I have worked with many women who live some version of this story. As a matter of fact, Milwaukee has one of the largest sex trafficking rings in America. I continue to come in contact with many young teens and women currently involved in some form of prostitution. After interviewing a number of them it became obvious the connection between all of them is their longing for

Desperately in Search of ...

their daddy's love. Many of them have developed a tough skin, appear hard and aggressive in a way so society fears them—but inside she is still that little girl who needs her father. I strongly believe this is another critical milestone: when she is transitioning from a teenager into a woman. She desperately searches for a father figure in order to define who she is and the woman she is trying to become. It is this father she seeks to identity with as she explores the various components of herself. If he is absent, she is vulnerable, and her heart is easily captured by the first man who pays attention even though he has no good intentions. When he further batters her heart, this man then sets the example of how she should expect to be loved and treated by a man.

It is important that fathers are there, so he recognizes when his little girl becomes interested in the opposite sex. If they have a strong bond, he will notice her sudden interest in things he is interested in. She may become more interested in sports or her daddy's career choice in an effort to look for a way to connect with him. It is this innate desire that helps her to define and understand the emotional connection she will later have with men. It is her father's guidance and affirmation she needs in order to develop into a young woman with a strong sense of confidence and self-worth. This father-daughter's love sets a tone for how she should be treated as a woman because of how her father treats her, and most important, her mother.

If this connection is absent, she becomes desperate, and will search for it in whatever way it presents itself to her. Because she is not able to make a sound judgment, she is often led by emotions and hormonal instability. In this search for love and validation, she is vulnerable because of her immaturity and the inability to value herself. As her hormones continue to surge and the sexual influences in society entice her, she seeks sexual attention from boys and men. As a result, she allows herself to be sexually exploited because it temporary satisfies the longing for a daddy's love.

Her mom may be able to temporally distract her with the mommy-daughter love. However, mommy will never contain the curiosity or her quest to be validated by her daddy. Her mother can only represent an example of what a woman should be, but she could never give her daughter the validation she needs to define who she is, and how she should be received. As the daughter grows up, she will seek her own interpretation of how she is to be valued as a woman. Because she is searching in desperation, her interpretation will never represent her value.

Once she has been violated by her misinterpretation, it validates the self-worthlessness she has already experienced as the result of feeling abandoned by her father. As she continues into womanhood with a false sense of her self-worth, she will evolve into a woman who becomes accustomed to hurt and shame. She grows accustomed to the repeated cycle of abandonment and abuse, and even if she manages to escape teen motherhood, engaging in risky behaviors, or self-exploited behaviors, she does not escape the harm due to lack of self-worth. She still searches for her father's love and validation through broken and abusive relationships and/or marriages.

I am not saying that all fatherless daughters will go on a path of self-destruction. What I am saying is that women who have been on that path are more likely to be fatherless. Although I believe fatherlessness is the main factor, there are many other factors, such as environment, upbringing, relationship with her mother, and other exposures. You can see that the two stories—mine and Josie's—appear to be very different, but were both young women who suffered as a result of fatherlessness. What connects us is the fact we both struggled with some of the same feelings of abandonment, lack of self-worth, and feeling unloved. Although our lives presented two different paths, we both grew up and became broken women lacking self-worth and self-love. We sacrificed as we settled into womanhood without our crowns.

In the next chapter, I will present my definition of what it means to be a woman without a crown as I share more of my journey of healing and self-discovery.

CHAPTER 6:

A Woman Without a Crown

Before she can understand how she should be loved as a woman, as a young girl she must first encounter the intimate experience of love from her father. It is through his love she learns the secrets to her self-love, self-worth, and self-validation. Therefore, he should be the first man who captures her heart. Once he captures her heart, she learns to wait for the one who is worthy enough to receive it.

A Woman Without a Crown

Who is she as she walks in the shadows, secretly struggling with knowing her worth, yet she shows herself to the world, pretending to be happy among them? I call her a woman without a crown, or a woman who has been broken. It is not easy to spot a broken woman because she becomes skilled at hiding herself. She is able to blend into her environment, appearing to hold it together without anyone knowing who she is or where she has been. On the outside, she looks like any other woman. She is the professional woman, Christian woman, rich woman, poor woman, Black women, Hispanic woman, White woman, educated woman, working woman—any woman. However, she has been broken.

Some of these women would never admit they are broken, and may even mask their brokenness by appearing mean or aggressive. No matter how the brokenness is displayed, underneath the mask, they are all the same. If her father has failed to capture her heart, she can't escape the brokenness, and she is vulnerable because she becomes a victim to everyone who is unworthy of her heart.

Because she has not been validated, she subconsciously defines herself as a woman without a crown and she learns to love in a broken heart. I call this the "broken-heart syndrome." Because her esteem has already been damaged, she is vulnerable as she blindly searches for some understanding of how she is to be loved. Because of this predisposition, she accepts when she is mistreated, and masks her pain as she goes on to establish her false sense of self.

Here I was broken as I found myself still waiting for my daddy's love to teach me something. I was a woman in my late thirties, I had accomplished many things, yet I realized I could benefit from my father's love and validation. As a broken woman, I was accustomed to masking my feelings, but inside of me was a young child longing for her father. While other girls dreamed of marrying Prince Charming, I believed he was out of my reach. It wasn't that I didn't think I was pretty enough, I felt I wasn't worthy enough because of my family secrets. Although I desired love, I limited myself to loving in my broken heart, and accepted a role as a victim as I desperately searched for something to validate me. I walked through life feeling ashamed, guilty, and unworthy, and no matter where the abuse came from, I believed I was supposed to just accept it.

It became a vicious cycle, because I learned to choose men who were emotionally unavailable, while secretly holding them to expectations they could never fulfill. Like many fatherless women, I found comfort in unhealthy relationships as I blindly chased after the love of my absent father. When I found myself at the brink of a relationship with a man without baggage, I didn't know how to stay in it, so I quickly bailed out before we got too close. I was afraid of blowing my cover, so I ended it and offered my friendship. I could stand being a good friend, but I would try not to get close enough for him to view me as a potential mate. If he pursued me, no matter how much I liked him, I would never make myself available.

I didn't believe I deserved to be with a man who was held in a high standing. Besides, the interactions between us were unfamiliar and unpredictable because he was squeaky clean—and he treated me like royalty. I admit I enjoyed the royal treatment as long as he did not expect anything beyond a simple date. I was fortunate to have dated some of the nicest men, but because I carried so much shame, I felt like they were in a league where I didn't qualify. However, on the outside, one would think I fit in the league, never knowing that inside I hid many broken pieces.

It was easy for me to identify with a man who kept me connected to the broken little girl from my past. It took a long time before I was able to realize I couldn't get the love fulfilled that I longed for from my father, through the abusive men I had been cycling through. I kept introducing them to the broken little girl who was abandoned by her father, expecting them to fix her. However, they received her only to bring more harm to her.

Everything but a king

My first broken relationship was with the father of my children. After two years away at school and running from a potentially good guy, I returned home. I was now in search of something to define me as a woman. I dated him because he had flaws, and was therefore a man I felt I was worthy of knowing. It was not his qualities that drew me to him, it was his imperfections. However, he appeared to have everything I longed for: had a mother and father, was upper middle-class, lived in a house in good neighborhood, and appeared to be normal. I ignored the fact he didn't finish high school, had a young son, was under employed, was a nonbeliever, and was farther from being prepared for adulthood than anyone I knew. However, I was trying to define myself as I entered in to womanhood and desperately needed someone to validate me. I also needed to escape my darkest secret: *loneliness*.

I allowed our relationship to move forward and I committed to being with him, no matter what. Despite how hard I tried to please him and his family, I was rejected. In their eyes, I was poor, orphaned, and could never be good enough for their son. I was emotionally abandoned in our marriage, and spent fifteen years pleading and begging for his love and acceptance. I was robbed of my voice and subjected to infidelity, physical and emotional abuse, mistreatment, and outright disrespect. I was paralyzed by fear and suffocated by guilt. Whenever I gathered enough strength to confront him, I was beaten, isolated, and abandoned for months on end. Once I was stripped to my core, emotionally mangled, and lonely, I would then plead for his return—and blame myself for the mistreatment.

This was the cycle of our marriage, and I never allowed myself to mourn my pain. I repeatedly patched up my face and adjusted my mask because I was determined to face the world with a smile on my face. As the years went by, I birthed son after son, exposing them to the abuse of their mother. When they grew older, it became a norm, and they unknowingly took part. If I dared to protest any unfair treatment, my sons became pawns and were literally snatched from my arms and taken from me until I was willing to submit. At times, I wasn't allowed to see them for several hours. Although it would only be short-lived, I was controlled by the fear of never seeing my children again. No matter how many earned degrees were now behind my name, I could never measure up to him and his family because I was deemed unworthy.

The saddest part: I believed it. I foolishly allowed myself to keep getting pregnant, beaten during my pregnancies, cheated on, and abandoned, thinking that one day he would see how much I loved him—and would one day love me back. While pregnant with my youngest son, I suffered many complications due to the loss of his twin. He was born at thirty-two weeks. I became preoccupied with the amount of care he needed. By the time I realized I had been abandoned again, I knew it was time for me to get out. With six young boys to care for, I gathered enough courage and filed for my divorce. However, I was unaware of the invisible chain I would wear around my neck for several years after.

I escaped my broken marriage, but I subconsciously continued to attract people who maintained my victim status. To cope with my loneliness, I became a rescuer, and allowed friends and family to take advantage of me by letting them move in and out of my home. I tried to take care of their needs when I needed to be taking care of the needs of my children and myself. I desperately wanted to be viewed as a woman deserving love.

About a year after my divorce, I began to date. Because I had not yet learned my self-worth, and again—I didn't allow myself to get close to any man who I felt was out of my league. If he was educated and established, loved the Lord, and was an all-around good guy, I thought he deserved a woman far more worthy than me. I would sabotage the relationship before it got too deep. I wore a mask to hide my shame because I never wanted this man, who I felt was out of my league, to be exposed to it. If they allowed me, I would remain a good friend and play it safe.

On the flip side, I would easily attach to men who identified with something from my past—often a man who was rough around the edges, struggled with their faith, had hidden aggression, minor criminal past, poor financial history, etc. I wasn't able to evaluate these clear red flags. However, the red flags were often very clear to those around me. When the pieces didn't match, many of my friends and family were bold enough to question my choices. I would exaggerate the man's economic stature or his moral values in an effort to appease my peers.

Here I was obligating myself into a relationship with a man who is emotionally abusive, and a great manipulator. The only thing we had in common was the fact we were both single parents, grew up poor, and came from an extremely large family. Yet I allowed myself to seek security within him, because although I was financially stable, this was familiar. I lacked the tools to evaluate the facts: he was ending his second marriage, was in his second foreclosure, couldn't keep a stable job, and was very aggressive and manipulating. Although I was not in a physically abusive relationship, I was emotionally, spiritually, and financial abused. I thought if I gave enough, loved enough, tried enough, I could fix him. In exchange, I would be free of the past abandonment because he would give me the love I was missing from my father.

It took me five years to realize this man was sinking me as he manipulated me into co-signing thousands and thousands of dollars in loans, credit cards, etc., to pay off his debt. At times, I was supporting both my children and his children, paying my own and his bills, too. To keep me victimized, he would become cold and verbally abusive, and sometimes emotionally abandoning. I even allowed him to blame me for his financial distresses, although they were present long before I entered the scene. He threw massive tantrums, yelled and screamed, broke things I valued, threatened to kill himself, and would not allow me to see his daughters, who I had come to love. While in this relationship, I lived in fear of him doing something crazy to himself. This is how he got me to surrender the money he wanted or the signature he needed for the loan. Once he got what he wanted, he appeared to be the most loving man—until his next point of desperation.

I allowed my voice to be stolen in circumstances where I truly needed to be heard. I tried desperately to get him to realize I loved him as I used my own finances to fix his mess. I allowed him to drag me into foolish investments, taking advantage of my kindness and abused heart. I became comfortable with who I had become, because my trade-off was concealing the shame of my lost identity. When I finally gathered enough strength to move on, he coerced me back with the wedding ring and promises I desperately desired. When I was seriously ill, and he emotionally abandoned me, I knew then it was time to end the relationship. However, I did not come out unharmed, as I was stripped of my financial security and was forced to file bankruptcy, and later lost my home. Like my other relationship, I didn't allow myself to feel any grief, as I again assumed this was just life, as I swallowed my pain, and moved on. I adjusted my mask to hide this new pain as I reconstructed my life and pretended it was all good.

A few months after I was recovering and out of the hospital, I was destined to put the pieces of my life back together. I met a man who claimed to be a true born-again Christian, and proclaimed his only motive was to live for the Lord. He was upfront and honest about his criminal background, had been out of prison for four years, and had reestablished himself financially and spiritually. Although I was open to a friendship, I informed him I was recovering from a long-term illness, and had just broken off an engagement after a five-year relationship. We begin to have long conversations over the phone about God and our desire to live for him. Before long, we were praying every morning and evening, and I felt a spiritual closeness to him I had never felt with anyone, especially a man. I became heavily focused on God's Word, and masked the abandonment and shame overwhelming me.

Because I was somewhat isolated from my family at that time, his friendship came along at the right moment. He was a great supporter when I unexpectedly took ill again, he immediately came to my rescue. I spent three additional weeks in the hospital. Although I tried to conceal my illness from him, his intrusion softened my protest. While I was in and out of conscious, I would hear him there praying for me. Sometimes he would be alone, other times with my friend or the few family members who visited. He spoke to the doctors and made major decisions about my health when I couldn't. While I was home recovering, he came over and took control over my personal affairs, had my roof replaced, took care of the kids, paid for groceries and small bills in exchange for nothing. At least that was what I thought.

As I regained my strength, he revealed he was in love with me, and he felt God had sent me to him. He explained he had been without a woman for a long time, and was ready to get married. I didn't know how to say no because he had taken such good care of me when I was ill, and had asked for nothing in return. However, he manipulated me into making a decision to marry him by shutting me out, and not speaking to me until I agreed to marriage, despite my desire to speak to my pastor. Within that week, I obligated myself, and we were quickly married, even though I had only known him for four months.

As in the past, I was not able to evaluate the relationship or read the red flags. However, I later realized he was the most like my father in the present day. He proclaimed to be a born-again Christian who was looking for a second chance at living right. The marriage was short-lived, as he assumed we would still live separately, and my role was only to satisfy his sexual urges upon his request. When I protested his arrangements, he abandoned me the day after we married, and avoided me for months until he finally agreed to file for divorce.

During that time, I contacted his family, his pastor, and anyone I remembered meeting through him. No one in his close circle was aware we were married, and he led them to believe we were no longer dating. This was when I discovered he had a history of being a womanizer—and an abuser. When I called him for answers, he became verbally abusive and threatened me. I was puzzled, because this was not the man who had catered to my every need over the last four months. Although I did not love him, I committed to the relationship because I felt obligated and was once again trying to love in a" broken heart". With his refusal to explain, I was left dumbfounded, hurt, embarrassed, and didn't know where to turn.

Something about "the third strike and you're out" must have registered with my emotional state. This last relationship hit me so hard I was left on the brink of an emotional overload. Because of embarrassment, I kept this marriage a secret, and didn't tell anyone other than my father. Although my father and I had an estranged relationship, we spent some time together during my illness. Prior to this, he always seemed self-absorbed and unavailable. However, I was emotionally broken and needed him to be emotionally available. At this moment, I just wanted this experience to be an opportunity for him to hold me in his arms and tell me everything would be okay. We had gotten closer, and I assumed that he would want to be there.

Instead of receiving the comfort I expected, I was greeted with criticism, rejection, and further abandonment. I felt stupid as he scolded me, judged me, and criticized me. I sat on the phone in silence, regretting I had ever attempted to reach out to him. My tears fell like a waterfall while I allowed him to demolish the remaining pieces of my battered heart. I didn't understand how a man could criticize his daughter for her faults when he was never there to give her any direction or guidance. I learned how to love through my pain, which started long before I desired a man. I couldn't believe how arrogant he was as he went on and on, forgetting it had been only about twelve years since he had gotten his life together. Once the phone conversation ended, I found myself on my knees crying out to God, asking for his help.

I met *all of Sonja* for the first time on that day when I begin to realize how broken I was, and how I had built my self-worth around whether or not I could fix broken men. I realized I subconsciously believed I deserved how life had treated me because I was born into it. Although I had managed to mimic a social-economic class, I always felt like an impostor because I carried the shame of my father and my mother. I was a pretender, and I fooled the world, but I couldn't fool God or myself. The reality: I connected with broken men because I needed a place where I didn't have to be the perfect woman I pretended to be in front of the world. In my professional life, my outer shell showcased a successful, confident, strong woman, but underneath the core was an abandoned and abused child, wanting to be loved. These relationships were a way I validated the lies I continued to feed myself.

"You are just not worthy of that kind of love, Sonja, because you were born unworthy." This was one of the biggest lies that I subconsciously told myself.

The hardest thing I ever had to do was to face the truth about my brokenness. So many people are afraid to admit they have hurt in their past, so they continue to repeat the same mistakes over and over again. However, I was at the point where I realized it, and all I could do then was stretch out my arms and cry out, "Lord, here I am stripped financially, emotionally, and physically, but I need you to help me through this. I thank you now because I know you will bring me through this pain."

The mere fact I wanted to face myself was tough, but when I did, everything in the world made sense. God began to show me myself, and I became aware of my own cycle as a broken woman as he reintroduced me to the little girl who had faced years of abandonment, loneliness, pain, and lack of self-worth. I was praising God because I know I had made progress because I was on my way to loving her, healing her, and crowning her. I knew then that God had a plan for my life, and it was time for me to stop running from it.

When we hold onto the unresolved hurt and abandonment, we subconsciously attach ourselves to people who will continue to reinforce it. Because we are broken, we become comfortable in our unhappiness, and accept it as our way of life. Broken people tend to attach to broken people, and in the dynamics of their relationship, one displays the role of the villain while the other acts as the victim.

In the next chapter, I will continue to talk more about how broken women cycle through relationships with broken men. I will touch on domestic violence and review some of the traits of both the victim and abuser. If you are in an abusive relationship, please contact your local agency dealing with domestic violence. No one deserves to be mentally, physically, emotionally, or sexually abused. You can also call 1-800-799-7233 or 1-800-787-3224 (TTY) for national domestic violence hotline.

CHAPTER 7:

Not in Search of a King

Liberation ...

When I first met you, you pretended to be a perfect guy.
Then I got to know you, and now I'm wondering why?
Why did I let myself love you thinking it would one day come true?
One day you would really love me. Oh, if I only knew!
Knew then what I know now, perhaps my heart could have been spared.
You have never cherished my devotion to you. Did you ever even care?
You only cared about yourself, and how you could be pleased.
You never intended to be my King; I was just your moment's tease.
When I gave up my hand to you, my heart masked the danger.
Once I really belonged to you, you became an unfamiliar stranger.
You acted like I meant nothing to you, except sometimes in bed.
One minute you use and abuse me, then feed empty promises in my head.
Then sometimes you would say, "I love you" Oh my word, what a joke.
Whenever those words escaped from your lips, I felt like I would choke.
How can you say you love me, and treat me as badly as you do?
If you believe in love, you know that your love in not true.
You see true love contradicts a broken heart and the pain I endured.
A blackened eye, a baby lost, and finances now unsecured.
It takes a true King to be willing to love his precious bride.
Allowing myself to be your Queen has shattered my womanly pride.
Goodbye I say to you today as I heal and set myself free.
Today God has given me a new day to fall in love with me.

When a woman is aware of her crown, she waits to be discovered by her king. She will not settle for anyone who is not worthy of her heart, because her father has made her aware of her worth. If a man is not prepared to treat her as well as her daddy does, she will not allow him to take a place in her heart. If she believes she was not good enough to be loved by her father, she will not think she is good enough to be loved by a man who has been raised to be king. Because she struggles with this emotional abandonment, she does not validate her own self-worth, and has not learned to set standards as she searches after love. If she never does any soul searching, she doesn't realize missing the love of her father has everything to do with whom she chooses as her mate.

A woman without a crown will search for love, but she will not search for a king. Instead of engaging in a healthy intimate relationship, she looks for broken relationships to fulfill the void left by her absent father. Because she is more likely to have been victimized in her childhood, she learns to submit to the victim stance, and will engage in codependent relationships with men unwilling to love her.

A codependent relationship is when you deny your own needs, and become fixated on the needs of others. The relationship is always off balance because it always consists of a giver and a taker.

Self-destructive relationship cycle

In many cases, the woman is not aware of her own self-destructive relationship cycle. She doesn't necessarily set out to search for a man to mistreat her, but she is searching for images that familiarized her with the pain associated with growing up fatherless. She:

- Is willing, because of this brokenness, to do anything for love, even going as far as self-sacrifice.
- Will settle in an unhealthy relationship, if she believes a man loves her, believing the mistreatment has to do with something she did or is not doing.

- Even when she is aware of it, she continues to subject herself to infidelity, abandonment, heartache, and abuse.
- May even blame herself and believe she can fix it by being a better woman, lover, friend, etc.
- Subconsciously becomes fixated on trying to fix the unsalvageable relationships, which are a direct connection to the broken bond between her and her daddy.
- Secretly cycles through the ups and downs of her life, and feels embarrassed in fear of being judged by her peers.
- May not be aware she is being victimized because she justifies his actions or emotionally detaches from them. If someone tries to force her to accept it before she is ready, she pushes them away while seeking comfort in the arms of the one who mistreats her.
- Continues to find comfort in her pain, and becomes immune to her suffering until something traumatic happens to awaken her.

When a daughter has a strong bond with her father and feels she is being mistreated; she is more likely to recognize the abuse earlier on and will seek refuge in her father.

Sabotaging good relationships

You are probably wondering why an emotionally broken woman wouldn't just go after the good guys. Well, you should know: it is not that the good guys never came along in my life. If fact, they were probably more accessible than the ones I selected. However, every time I was introduced to a man who had the potential of treating me well, I ran because I feared the unknown, I knew how to stay in an unhealthy relation but not how to stay in a potentially good relationship, because it was unfamiliar, and I felt uncomfortable.

With a king, I found myself feeling restless, anxious, and subconsciously waiting for his abandonment as I searched for an exit. It's not because I didn't want to be with him, I just didn't believe I deserved him so I would befriend him, but I was afraid to commit. He tried hard to prove himself, but I would never give up anything more than a gentle hug or firm handshake. The more he tried, the more I subconsciously sabotaged the relationship. I ended up hurting many of them because I simply did not know how to love a king. Although my heart longed for all he offered, a part of me felt I was not worthy. I felt unworthy because I was ashamed of my fatherlessness, and didn't want to be judged because of this.

Understanding domestic abuse

I never recognized my own victimization until I was ready to face myself. When I begin to search within myself, I discovered many abandonment issues held me captive and subjected me to my victimization cycle. Although I tried to hide it, my personal tragedies were continuing to contradict my professional life until I was ready to do my emotional healing. The more I was mistreated, the more I gave of myself in an effort to keep them from harming me. I was never able to focus on my own happiness because I was afraid of reliving the traumatic feeling of abandonment. Because I was not aware of my emotional cycle, I lived my life recovering from abuse and abandonment. I kept losing more and more of myself, thinking that one day he would stop using me, mistreating me, and abusing me. When one relationship ended, I would enter the next abusive relationship, depleted and becoming familiar with the victim role. I would convince myself I had it figured out—and this time I would get it right. I became invested in trying to repair a situation that was beyond repair, yet I believed if I gave enough, loved enough, or worked hard enough, I would finally be loved. As a result, I had fallen from my commitment to my faith; I lost my financial security, and many material things, dreams, and desires. When I was able to be honest about my past, I was ready to work toward my healing.

It was when I participated in a women's support group for victims of domestic violence, I began to understand what I had actually been through. It wasn't that I needed to identify with the victimization as much as I needed to make sense of the reality of it. Prior to this self-discovery, I could never figure out why I wasn't comfortable working with women who were victims of domestic violence. I would refer them out because I was too disconnected from the subject, and it was too close for comfort. Today I have become an advocate, and I am able to provide therapy and support to these women.

A few years ago, a friend was in an abusive relationship. This was the first time I had a personal encounter with domestic violence outside of a victim's stance. I reached out to help her, but I was unable to convince her she needed to leave. One night I wrote my experience in my journal. "I now find myself in an awkward situation as I wait on the other side. I can't help but wonder if she would have the courage to get out. She is going through domestic violence, and there is nothing I can do to convince her to break free. I feel her slipping through my fingers as my heart aches from her pain."

The frustration came because one minute she is calling in a panic because she fears for her safety after he had struck her. Yet when she was on the verge of leaving, just when I thought I had her convinced, and we reviewed the escape plan, she pulls out and says, "Don't call the house. We are good now. I decided to stay." I was suddenly shut out and left to worry about her safety until she resurfaced weeks later. I had no choice but to respect her wishes because I didn't want to set him off. I was also angry because I know what "we are good now" means. It means they have entered a false honeymoon period, and either he has frightened her to where she feels paralyzed, or has manipulated her into believing he is going to change. The reality is: unless the abuser gets the help he needs and acknowledges his faults, he will never change. He will only get worse as he gains more control.

"How do you help someone when they don't want to leave, even when they are in danger? How could I be mad at her when I was her?"

Although I wanted to help her, I knew the only thing I could do is give her the resources, be a listening and non-judgmental ear, and be there when she is ready to make her escape. I understood her stance, because at one time, I secretly stood in the same circumstances, not saying a word to anyone. At least she had the courage to reach out and to call someone. I prayed for her hoping next time she would have the courage to leave. Fortunately, several months later, it happened again, and she did get out.

Victims tend to feel paralyzed in an abusive situation because it may appear as if she has no way out. Even if there is a clear road in front of her, if she is not ready to emotionally stand without him, he will keep snatching her back. He preys on the little girl inside of her who is longing to be loved by her daddy. This is not to say every fatherless daughter will be a victim of domestic violence. However, I believe it is more likely for women who felt abandoned by their fathers to struggle with self-worth, which is a characteristic of victims of domestic violence. Therefore, it is my professional assumption that a daughter who grows up without her father's validation is at a greater risk. Because she hasn't found her self-worth, the man who abuses her is the only security she has, and she will stay in the relationship. Just because she appears to be comfortable, doesn't mean she doesn't long for what she sees in other relationships. She has convinced herself she will one day win his love. For this reason, she continues to sell her soul to him, even though she knows he isn't worthy of her love. This man is well aware of her battered heart—and uses it at his advantage.

Once she becomes attached, it is difficult for her to let go because of her desperation to seek love from him. It's important to understand a woman in an abusive relationship may not be able to get out right away. She has already invested so much that she will hold on, and go to any extent to protect it. Because she has not yet found herself, she doesn't realize the love she desires will never come from anyone *until she learns how to love herself.*

This is such a serious topic, and it is important to spend some time talking about domestic violence as it relates to fatherless daughters. Is a woman, who has not been validated by her father, more likely to fall victim to domestic abuse? No one is immune to domestic violence. It occurs in all social and economic groups, races, genders, ages, and classes, and is not just limited to physical abuse. However, many don't want to acknowledge they are victimized because they often want to protect their abusers or fear them.

It isn't by consequence that a broken woman ends up in the hands of an abuser. He knows exactly how to spot his victim because he pays close attention to the relationships surrounding her, especially the one with her father. When he discovers the daddy role is inactive, he pretends to be her savior by providing all she has longed for. The common mistake she makes is letting him preview her weaknesses as well as her feelings of abandonment left by her father. The abuser preys on these weaknesses, and will use them against her. Once he captures her heart, he isolates her, and her fairytale quickly fades. He will blame her for the abuse, and she believes fixing his problems would make the situation better.

In the next few paragraphs, I will give examples of the various forms of abuse. I am speaking from my own point of view as both a professional and former victim. I experienced these forms of abuse: physical, verbal, sexual, emotional, and financial.

Physical abuse

It is never okay for anyone to be slapped, hit, punched, pushed, restrained, or bitten. Regardless of why it occurs, it is all physical abuse. This is the worst form of abuse because it usually progresses and can lead to serious injuries and death. It often starts with physical restraints; then draws a fine line to abuse, and includes, for example: holding you down, squeezing your mouth, sitting on you, etc. Once he gets physical and gets away with it, he knows he can continue because he has broken your spirit. Each time it occurs, it gets more intense as he has the need to gain even more control. Like you, he wears his masks. In front of the world, he appears to be the gentlest man, but behind closed doors, you see the face of a vicious monster. As long as he knows you will keep his secrets, it becomes the norm, and he continues to use it as a way of controlling you.

Not in Search of a King

Because of my own abandonment issues, I mistook the initial overbearing control as a form of love and attention. When I was being physically abused, I was convinced it was something I did to bring it on. "Maybe I shouldn't have questioned him when he can in at 2 a.m." I allowed myself to experience domestic abuse while pregnant with my children. On one occasion, I was punched, slapped, and choked until I passed out.

Although many of these incidents occurred well over fifteen years ago, I was not able to admit having experienced them until I finally faced myself a few years ago. I don't know how I managed to mask it all, and go on with life without ever telling anyone. I stayed in this relationship for a very long time because I held on for the honeymoon period, where he appeared remorseful, and gave our future a false sense of promise. For some reason, that gave me comfort. However, it was short-lived, because a new incident was often a reminder that kept me in fear. Although I can recall some pretty severe incidents, I never associated it with the possibility I could be seriously injured, lose my life, or my children be emotionally damaged by what they witnessed. Although some of my boys were affected, I thank God I made it out of that situation because there are many women who never do.

Verbal abuse

Most of us don't really understand verbal abuse. On some level, almost everyone has experienced it. However, we don't always recognize it as a form of abuse. Verbal abuse is when someone yells, screams, uses insults, name calling, threatening tones, or verbal threats to get you to submit to their will. My encounters with verbal abuse occurred far more frequently and more recently than physical abuse. After many years of dealing with physical abuse in the first marriage, I convinced myself I was in a better situation because he never hit me. However, he used insults, empty threats, silent treatment, occasionally called me the "B" word, and repeatedly yelled. Whenever I tried to have a voice later proved to be no better. I would shut down and respond with a blank stare because his words came too fast. I silently surrendered because

I couldn't think of anything to say in his fit of rage. To him, it appeared I was being defiant, and he would become more intense, screaming one insult after the other without ever taking a breath. "I know what you trying to do." "You are trying to play games with me." "You know exactly what I'm talking about." "Why are you messing with me?" "What, you think you are better than me?"

This went on sometimes for days until I finally submitted and then he blamed me for the argument. I never got to say much of anything when he was like that, but somehow I allowed him to convince me it was my fault. I learned quickly how to soothe him when I saw he was on the verge of a tantrum. Sometimes I was able to calm him down by giving in right away. However, when I wasn't able to immediately respond, he would lose it. I felt like I was walking on eggshells, and was always on alert because I never knew when I was going to put out an emotional fire.

Sexual abuse

Anytime someone forces you or pressures you into a sexual act you are not agreeing to, it is sexual abuse. It is difficult to accept that sexual assault occurs within a marriage or intimate relationship. However, it does. Who wants to view the person they love as someone who is sexually exploiting you? Especially when he has convinced you that you knew what was happening, liked it, and wanted it. Many women don't realize they have a right to say no to sex when they are not comfortable with it, even if they are in a marriage. Because of what was happening, I hated intimacy, sex, and anything associated with it. However, I submitted to it, was forced to do it, and accepted it. It didn't know sex was something I was supposed to enjoy, as much as I assumed it was supposed to be taken.

Because of the unresolved childhood sexual abuse, I felt uncomfortable with sexual intimacy in the past. I would emotionally disconnect from the physical act when I felt pressured to do it. I felt violated when I found myself wakened out of my sleep to him engaging in intimacy with me after I had been hurt by him.

The last thing I wanted to be was close to him. However, I said nothing as I lay there, pretending I was still asleep, and allowed him to continue. I hated him during those dreadful moments, but by morning those feelings faded and I pretended to be ok. I lived with this for years, never admitting I was being abused, because I convinced myself it was something men were allowed to do. After all, I was committed to him and belonged to him.

Even after obligating myself into this new relationship, I carried my broken self with me and wasn't able to realize he too was broken. After vowing to celibacy until remarriage, I was manipulated and pressured into breaking my vow. Before long, I found myself caving in until I had fully submitted to what I believed was living in sin. To avoid the arguing and fear of abandonment, I submitted even though my heart was filled with guilt and shame. Once I had invested several years, I became numb and avoided the situation whenever I could.

Emotional abuse

Sometimes it is not always easy to recognize emotional abuse because of the manipulation, where someone uses intimidation, guilt, aggression, and promises, to control your actions. This abuser preys on your emotions, and uses people dear to you to keep you controlled. For example, he may promise you marriage, a baby, a big house, or anything to keep you roped in. However, he has no intentions of fulfilling those promises, and will somehow find a way to discard them. He will manipulate you into agreeing to do things that benefit him by being deceptive, charming, aggressive, throwing a fit, lying, etc. One of the most forms of control is the shut-out technique. He emotionally abandons you because he knows this is what you fear the most and when he's ready, you will accept him back. It is a way of manipulating your abandonment issue you already have from your absent father. You become his yo-yo, and his motive is to keep you in a vulnerable position so he can always get what he wants when he wants it.

I experienced emotional abuse in all of my unhealthy relationships.

Because my biggest fear was abandonment, I was a major people pleaser, which my abusers were all skilled at detecting. I allowed myself to be manipulated into an unwanted debt, a marriage I was not ready for, and many other things. Whenever I tried to confront the abuse, something I valued would be stripped from me, and dangled over my head. Because I would be so desperate, I was in an emotional fog, and would eventually submit to the demands of my abuser. It did not matter if it was giving up my celibacy, writing out a check, signing a loan, or accepting mistreatment; I gave in because I needed to be relieved from the emotional abandonment. What I did not realize at the time was I never had any relief; it was just a superficial coating to sooth my pain.

Financial abuse

The financial abuse was something new to me because I had never heard of such a thing. However, it is real and becoming more common. I don't think financial abuse can occur without other forms of abuse being present first. A financial abuser is a person who intentionally abuses your financial situation. It doesn't matter if it is manipulating you to surrender cash, sign a loan or line of credit, or take out credit card. If someone is pressuring or manipulating you into doing any financial act where they benefit, it is financial abuse. If he is always trying to gain something financially from you, chances are he's a financial abuser. He may fool you into believing you are doing this *for the both of you,* when actually you are doing it only for him. If he is comfortable letting you carry the load, and has no desire to do anything to advance himself, he may get a temporary job, but it is never long lasting, or if he always makes excuses when it comes to paying you back, it's financial abuse. This person who says he loves you, pressures you and threatens to leave you if you don't give in. He may even convince you it's your fault because you won't give him the money. He may say things like, "If you don't give me the money, I'm going to lose my car, house, my kids," "I'm doing this for us," etc. He will continue to prey on you until you cave in.

I was in this relationship with this greedy man who lived in my pockets for over five years. I did not see it at first, until he started tracking my paychecks and money I was trying to save. However, by the times I realized what I had been forced into, I had taken out loans, credit cards, and signed off on bogus investments. I started to hide any extra money because otherwise he would hound me for it. I couldn't escape the yelling and screaming, as well as the suicidal threats coming rapidly at me when I contested. After finally committing to one loan and surrendering my personal information, more credit cards begin to surface. When I confronted him with the situation, he told me he would take care of it. When weeks and months went by, and I tried to bring up the topic, he would throw fits, accuse me of not trusting him, and then turn everything around, blaming it all on me. He also used his darling daughters as pawns because he knew how much I adored them.

At the end of this relationship, my credit was in ruins, and I was forced to file. Once my finances were depleted, his love for me changed, and he seemed unconcerned about my well-being. It took several years for me to recover from the repercussion of this relationship, and the daily reminder of my financial distress only made the feelings more intense.

No one deserves to be hurt emotionally, physically, sexually, financially, etc. Any form should be reported to your local police department or your local agency that works against domestic violence.

My professional recommendation is victims of domestic violence should seek counseling so they can be empowered, and also learn to recognize the signs of abuse. It's not your fault, and despite what he says, you don't deserve this. You cannot fix him, get him to stop abusing you, or make him love you. All you can do is heal yourself. Don't get caught up in the honeymoon period, because it is not long lasting. If you go back, you will give him more control, not that he has harmed you, and gotten away with it because you accepted him back. When you get out, please be sure that you take the time to heal your wounds; otherwise you will find yourself either back with the same abuser or in another abusive relationship.

Until you address your past, you will continue to be drawn to men who are capable of resurrecting the feeling of abandonment left by your absent father. Broken people have the tendency to be drawn to what is familiar. It's easy to believe it when he says he's sorry and will never hurt or wrong you again. However, if he does it once, he will do it twice, etc. When you get the courage to break free, make sure you stay free.

I now realized I had been carrying the "traits of a victim" in every relationship I entered. Although I was clueless in the past, once I made myself aware of these traits, I was able to read the "red flags," and recognize a potential abuser. Because many of you still are not aware, it is also important to list both the traits of a victim and the traits of an abuser. With what traits do you identify?

Traits of a victim:
- Constantly find yourself giving endlessly in order to gain love
- Have little value in your self-worth, and deny your own needs
- Avoid the reality of your pain by pretending life is okay
- Make excuses for your mate's abusive behaviors by blaming yourself
- Feel that your relationship is imbalanced, and you are unable to demand fair treatment
- Are overwhelmed with shame and guilt for victimization because of how you are being treated
- Feel powerless and not heard or validated
- Feel controlled and unable to have freewill over your own life
- Have unexplained sickness, headaches, digestive problems, physical injuries, etc.
- Feel stuck or trapped (like there is no life outside of him)
- Feel like you are walking on eggshells (afraid of upsetting him)

Traits of an abuser:
- Won't allow you to have your own voice
- Refuses to validate your needs

- Keeps you in fear of disappointing him
- Forces you to give up your friendships and to live isolated
- Refuses to trust you outside of his radar, always accusing you
- Is jealous of everything you do outside of him
- Needs to be in control of everything you do
- Criticizes everything you do, and constantly put you down
- Is very explosive and easily angered
- Throws child-like tantrums when he doesn't get his way
- Manipulates you into doing something you don't want to do
- Blames you or others for his inappropriate behaviors
- Is self-absorbed and self-centered, and nothing matters outside of him

A conversation with my mom

My mom, who was also a victim of domestic violence, called me the other night. Although she still struggles with schizophrenia, she happened to have a brief moment of sanity. She asked me what I was doing, and I told her that I was working on my book. When she asked me what I was writing about, I told her I was working on my chapter on domestic violence. She said, "You know, your dad use to beat me when we were together."

I said, "I know. I remember some of it because it happened when I was a little girl."

She paused for a moment and said, "I should write a book, because I really have a story to tell." She then started making rambling statements that didn't make sense, and then denied that she was abused, and rushed me off the phone. My mom often has brief moments where she will almost appear to be normal. However, whenever she encounters any traumatic memory, she gracefully transitions back into being mentally ill. It is easier for her to claim insanity than face her inner truth.

For more information about the red flags of domestic violence, visit the websites listed below:

www.relationshipredflags.com
www.newhopeforwomen.org/red-flags-for-domestic-abuse
www.knowtheredflags.org

CHAPTER 8:

Am I Not Your Daughter?

Fatherless ...

Who am I, but a lonely girl unfamiliar with her name?
Many missing pieces to my puzzle and a life rippled with shame.
My daddy didn't protect me because he wasn't around to know.
My life was headed straight for trouble all because he let me go.
Many nights I cried for him, wishing he could be there.
I needed to be his little princess, but he didn't seem to care.
I didn't understand what was happening, so I forced it all within.
I couldn't say, "Daddy" left me, because the tears would have no end.
I sucked it up and moved forward for it hurt too much to look back.
I buried my feelings in my chest, and carried my pain on my back.
When danger came to find me, and fear dwelled up inside,
I couldn't run to my daddy so I ran into my soul to hide.
I hid inside my own world, and lost myself in time.
I lost my innocence through my pain, but I never lost my mind.
Daddy didn't come to save me from what the evil men had done.
I was molested, and abused long before my life had begun.
I grew up feeling empty, and had no pride within.
I attracted to men who hurt me, only to live my past again.
My life became a cycle that at first I didn't understand.
If my daddy didn't love me, how can I expect it from a man?
Then I realized at that moment I had only done my best.
How can a girl become a strong woman when she was fatherless?

Several months ago I assumed I was just about finished writing the book—and my healing, and then it happened.

"Don't move, it's him," my friend whispered. I received the shock in her eyes as she glanced at an image approaching from behind me. My innate curiosity struggled to obey. However, I trusted her; I followed her instructions and sat quietly as I waited for the moment to pass. Finally it was over, and as he appeared in view, I got a glance of his side view as I sat nestled in my corner, praying he didn't look back. It was my father walking by our table as he was being directed to his seat. My heart raced, and a sudden wave of panic flooded my body, and not one inch of me escaped the experience. "Go to the car, I'll take care of the check," she said quickly as she searched for a solution that would bring comfort to me.

I quickly gathered my bag and my coat, and ran out the door before he could notice my presence. I shook so intensely I couldn't get my car door open. I laid my bag and coat across the car and rested on the hood as I took a deep breath. It was as if this panic attack had taken over my mind, body, and spirit. I didn't understand where this was coming from because I thought I was over him. However, on this day, I realized *I was still emotionally wounded*. I had a little more healing to do. This was the first time I had physically seen my father in almost three years, and it sent me into panic. I didn't know what he would say or do if he saw me because this encounter was a year after he would have received my letter, to which he had never responded. I quickly reminded myself I wasn't the little girl who was abandoned by him or the broken woman emotionally wounded by him. I was now a strong woman advocating for fatherhood, and his words could no longer wound me. Then I could breathe again, regained my composure, and was on my way. I knew then I needed to prepare myself for the next encounter with my father.

After speaking with so many fatherless daughters, I was taken aback by the emotional scars we all have in common. I had become aware of the fatherless epidemic and the connection to the common root of so many other issues. Many women are unknowingly hurting themselves as they desperately search for their father's love. I realized I had to write this book, not to get back at my father, but because I needed to heal, bring awareness, and help other women heal. Although I wasn't quite ready to face my father, I was ready to face the abandonment left by him. Three years has passed since the phone conversation when my father scolded my choices. However, I could still recall his words, and the pain I felt on that day. Perhaps he has avoided me because deep down inside he knew I had been wounded by him. I honestly don't think my father was concerned about how much more pain he was causing, as much as he was about me knowing I had really messed up. Every moment of the scolding felt like rubbing alcohol on an open wound. I wanted to stop my father before he went too far, but I was too broken to respond. I silently listened as my heart remained open to the emotional battering. I hung up the phone, fell to the floor, and I cried and cried for days before I was ready to face the reality of my brokenness.

Before I could respond to my father, I asked God to show me where it all began. Through tears and prayer, God walked me back through my life to that forgotten little girl. I had to be reintroduced to her so I could defend her when I confronted my father. I realized I was still connected to this little girl chasing after her daddy's heart. I had been holding unresolved pain, and needed to let go so I could emotionally heal. In order to do that, I needed to find my truth, and let my father know about this little girl who had been abandoned by him.

This is the letter I sent my father over a year after our phone conversation. At first, I was afraid of his response, but now that I am healed, I wait for it. However, I realize I said everything I needed to say in this letter, and he has every right to accept or reject it.

Am I Not Your Daughter?

※※※

Dear _____ (my father's first name),

Am I not your daughter? I just want you to take a moment and think about this question before you continue to read this letter. I called you in desperation because I was seeking comfort, love, and reassurance as I exposed broken pieces of myself to you. I found myself devastated by yet another bad relationship, and I needed my father to help me put the pieces back together. I don't know why I reached out to you, I just did. You were the first person with whom I shared this most heartbreaking moment. However, I didn't get what I had expected from you. Instead I felt scolded, criticized, and abandoned. I desperately needed to hear you say you were there, you'd say a prayer for me, or you would come by and check on me later. Any little encouragement would have eased the pain in my heart.

Out of respect for you, I listened silently while you continued breaking my heart in pieces. Tears soaked my clothes as they poured out without you even noticing. For the first time in my life, I felt a wave of unexplainable emotions. Instead of feeling loved by you, I felt attacked and angry as you insulted me. Your ten-minute conversation felt like hours in a torture chamber.

At that time, I didn't know how to react to you or express what I was feeling. I was beyond broken. You went on and on as you failed to realize I could only love how I learned to love. I didn't know any better because you were never there to show me better. After hanging up the phone, I fell to my knees and asked God to show me the source of my flaws, give me the courage to face myself, and help me heal. I isolated myself from everyone, and pondered over this because my healing did not come right away.

For weeks after our conversation, I felt shamed by you, and couldn't stop replaying your words in my head. "You are getting too old to keep making these same mistakes." "It seems like you would be wiser by now." "People start to wonder what wrong with you." "You can't read the red flags?" "Isn't this the third time you made this mistake?"

However, as time went on, God begin to deal with me. Before I knew it, I embarked on a journey that helped me realized who I was, where my downfalls begin, and why I allowed myself to continue in a repeated cycle of mistreatment and abuse. While on my journey, I begin to write. As I wrote, I was able to expose many heartbreaking moments, and realized I was still a little girl chasing after the love of her father, you.

When you scolded me, I felt like I was being abandoned all over again. Although I was a grown woman, I needed you to tell me life would be okay, and you were there to comfort me. I realized that as a father you were emotionally unavailable. For the first time in my life, I found myself mourning the years of abandonment, and I cried and cried as I replayed my life, viewing all the scenes where you were absent. As an adult, I was still secretly waiting for your love, and needed you to teach me something. For years, I hid my shame, pain, and loneliness as I silently desired to be one of your little princesses. I wanted my daddy to love me enough to come back and protect me.

As a young girl, I was haunted by my reflection of myself, which mirrored your image. I am my father's daughter, no doubt. I can't stop the tears from flowing because I am overwhelmed with the heartache of my reality. Wow! I am truly fatherless, and I spent all of my life searching for you, even when you physically stood in my presence. When you reentered my life, I thought for once the love I needed would be complete. Although I was a woman approaching her thirties, I secretly longed for your love, protection, and validation. However, I remained incomplete because I didn't have the courage to tell you what I needed, and you didn't seem interested in making yourself emotionally available.

I have so many things to address in this letter. First, I must answer this question for you. Why do I keep associating myself with men who prey on me, and take advantage? It was easy for them to do so because I already had a wounded heart that was never mended. This was the life I was born into, and because of your absences I was destined to be brokenhearted. While growing up fatherless, I learned to mask my pain, and move on until I found myself stumbling into the hands of one abuser after the next. I realized I was caught in a vicious cycle of trying to repair the emotional abandonment that had stuck to me when you left long ago. Although I was searching for love, I didn't know what love was if it hit me in the face. I knew how it felt to be abandoned, and I wanted to do all I could to stop it from happening, but a part or me kept drawing me to it. This may sound crazy, but it is true. I was drawn to men who reminded me of you. I tried to fix them so I could heal the little girl who was hurting inside. Instead I only caused her further injury.

Next question, what happened to the promises you made to me while you were in prison? You said you loved me, and when you got out, you were going to be a father to us, as this was a chance to start over. I waited almost ten years for you, with the hope I'd have a daddy when you got out. I wrote to you and kept you encouraged, hopeful, and loved, even though you did not deserve it. I was one of the little girls that you abandoned; yet I was the only one who reached out to you while you were confined.

As soon as you were free, your commitment to me became a faded memory as you decided to marry a woman in another state, only to later leave her brokenhearted. You tried to justify your reasons for abandoning her by saying she was some desperate woman who rushed marriage on you. I now understand her because a man like you came along— and I became her.

Then you scolded me as if you were puzzled your daughter would grow up and make dumb mistakes. Did you ever imagine that? Yet you judged me because of my poor choices in men. How can you see me, and not see a mere reflection of the women from your past. Yes, I did make poor choices in men, but it was you I've been chasing after. Although God forgives us of our sins, remember there are always consequences as a result of them.

I never got to tell you how hurt I was when you announced you were moving back to Milwaukee. I convinced your other daughters to be open to a relationship with you, and we all opened up, expecting more than you offered. You reentered my life when I was emotionally reliving the life of a young girl who had desperately awaited her father. This time he promised her he was coming. However, he came physically but emotionally—he has yet to arrive. You were physically present from time to time, but you were never emotionally committed to being my father. I did not let myself feel the disappointed, so I continued to search for my identity as a wife and mother, even though I was never my daddy's daughter.

Today is the first time I acknowledged that anger existed. As I write, I am still trying to figure out what to do with it. I'm angry because any major life events forcing emotions to go beyond the surface, you are once again, gone. You then waited in the distance until enough time had gone by for me to reabsorb the pain. You have never had to be a father to any of your own children. However, I often watched as an outcast, as you portrayed the best father to my stepbrother and stepsister. They even had the privilege of getting the best of you, and calling you Dad when I never did. Although I was in my late twenties when you married your fourth wife, it hurt that you had done so before repairing a relationship with us.

I am forced to be honest with you and myself if I desire to heal. I was always afraid if I confronted you, you would abandon me again. I realized you had already emotionally abandoned me. When you came back into my life, you introduced yourself by your first name, and it was apparent you did not come to be daddy. I was forced to face the world without you, and it wasn't fair. I didn't know how to protect myself, love myself, or be myself. I wanted to please you, love you, and be held in your arms. When I was a little girl and afraid, I created an image of you in my head and I sought comfort within it. I pretended you would come and recue me from the bad things that hurt me.

Until recently, I found myself still covering up for you, pretending you are the perfect father, yet that is something I have not gotten to experience. I lied for you, and made life easy for you. You never had to explain the memories I had of you beating my mother, why you killed my stepmother, why you were in prison, or why you choose not to be there for me. You asked me why I wasn't smart enough to see the red flags in my relationships. Your absence taught me how to accept abandonment—and how to and seek it out. Despite how beautiful I could make myself on the outside, it was hard to believe it internally.

Do you really know who I am? I was never as strong as I appeared to be. When you reentered my life, I had already perfected my mask and pretended to be intact. Do you know I have carried this sadness in my heart all of my life? Do you know how long I cried for you? I don't understand a lot of things about you, but I never judged you. I can count on one hand the times I felt you were trying to be a father. However, this hurt cuts deep, and it is why we would all step back and shut down. You let it go without trying to repair any of the damage. You have expected me to navigate through life without flaws when I had to raise myself. It breaks my heart when you forget I am your daughter.

You were the first man who was supposed to hold your four little daughters hearts. Instead, you were the first man to break our hearts. Some of us struggled more than others, but we all suffered from your absence. It's most painful I have no good memories of you in my childhood. I have lived in shame because I did not want people to know where I came from. I hated growing up without you. I always felt like I had no identity. I would be wrong to say you did not set an example for me. You did. Unfortunately, it wasn't the best example for me to follow. I spent the majority of my life seeking out relationships that would lead to hurt and abandonment. I would even accept mistreatment and abuse because I remember my mother taking it.

Although you were not there, you taught me I wasn't worth anything to you. My value was next to nothing, and it was okay for the man I love to abuse, abandon, and mistreat me. I have very vivid memories of you physically abusing my mother. I was very young, but I remember many of the incidents, and I remember being stricken with fear. At seven, I lost my mother to a mental illness.

As I approached 18, I was in search of something to define me, I desperately needed my father. I fell into a deep depression because I realized time was up, and my dream of being your little girl had ended. I felt worthless, unloved, ashamed, and tried to commit suicide because I couldn't imagine going into adulthood with you.

Do you know when my mom was ill we had no place to go? My sisters and I needed you there to protect us from the mistreatment we have all experienced throughout our childhood. Sometimes I would feel overwhelmed with sadness because our family is still very separated and broken. All I ever wanted was your love and validation. How can you expect us to come together when we all grew up so scattered? At times, we can go for months without speaking to one another. However, in front of a crowd, we pretend to be a most loving family. Yet many of our relationships with each other are superficial, and anything beyond the surface is nonexistent. My sister and I never learned the meaning of true love because we didn't have you or our mother to teach us. After our mother took ill, we were never together as a family again.

All of your questions and comments prompted me to write because I could not voice it to you at that time. You told me people are beginning to think something is wrong with me. I realized it's very true. Something was wrong with me. It wasn't until you mentioned it did I realize it was time to face my reality of my fatherlessness. I have been lonely all of my life. Not because I needed a man, but because I needed you. I missed you in my life, and needed your love to teach me how to be a woman with pride, self-worth and self-love. Because you weren't there, I was forced to enter major stages of life wearing a blindfold.

No one ever taught me anything about men and relationships. I never knew which men to stay away from, how I should expect a man to treat me, or when to look at the red flags. Not one could teach me that but you. Because you were not there to protect me, I was subjected to abuse and misuse. Your guidance would have shielded me from the pain I have passed down to my own children. I spent my life trying to replace the love I longed for from you. The only pure love I have experienced is the love of innocence from my own children. As a parent, I was blessed with the opportunity to experience unconditional love, which is perhaps why I have continued to reach out to you. I love you and always will because you are my father. I use to be ashamed to admit I was hurting and missed your presences.

I have tried to reach out to you over the years, but I don't think you understood what I needed from you. You may feel it is too late—the damage is already done. However, I have children who now long for a real relationship with their grandfather. They need someone they could be proud to call grandpa. Because of my mistakes, their father is not the man he needs to be for them. You are the only living grandfather they will have for the rest of their lives.

In closing, I know we haven't spoken since our last conversation. However, today I still desire my father's love and hope one day our relationship can grow beyond the surface. I have to admit I was hurt, but your response changed my life by forcing me to really look at myself, and face my past. This heartbreak helped me face the unhappiness I had been masking all of my life. I don't think I would be writing a book if I didn't have that conversation with you. As I went on my journey of self-discovery, I begin to dig deep and peel back the layers. The healing began to flow, and I stand today releasing the last piece of pain unto you. I can say I forgive you, and I am ready to move into a positive direction.

I can assure you, the world, and most of all, myself, I will never allow myself to be another victim. I have broken out of my cocoon and found my wings. Today I am ready to fly as I share my story and help many fatherless women find healing. I pray you are ready for what God has revealed to me. My book is not about pointing the finger. Most important is the healing that is needed to come through it. Today I am ready to stand in my truth. I hope you too will stand with me so the healing for our family can take its course. I know we cannot have the relationship I longed for as a young girl. However, I am open to creating a new relationship with my father.

I do understand if you are not able to do this. It takes a lot to look back over your life, and face the mistakes made. I pray God gives you the courage to do so, and you receive this message with an open heart and mind. I pray you will use what you have learned as a tool to teach other fathers you influence about the importance of bonding with their young daughters and sons. Perhaps you can share my story with them, letting them know how valuable a father's love is to his daughter. I hope you encourage them to stand up and be strong in their roles as fathers.

Signed, A daughter desperately seeking the love of her father

As time goes on, I think of my father every now and again. My children still ask about him, and sometimes this saddens me and I'm praying one day things will be different. Honestly, I have found peace in knowing I have voiced my truth. It wasn't about what he did with it, as much as it was about him hearing it. Perhaps he, too, was wounded, and is not able to face his own past. This may be why it is easy for him to disconnect from his children. I know my father grew up with both parents in the home. However, I'm not sure how functional it was. Even if my father never had the courage to read this letter, because it is in this book, it will always be available to him.

PART III:

Mending the Pieces

Chapter 9:
In Search of Her Crown.

Chapter 10:
How Does she Forgive Him, and Them?

Chapter 11:
She Crowns Herself Queen.

Chapter 12:
A Queen in Waiting

I am excited about this shift in our journey. Now that you have acknowledged the pain, it is time to mend the pieces. When I found healing, I found peace. The next four chapters walk you through my healing process. If you are ready to heal, I pray that you will end this section with the healing and peace that God has blessed me with. I created the workbook In Search of Your Crown to help guide you through the process.

CHAPTER 9:

In Search of Her Crown

She Finally Found Her Crown

Broken, battered, and abused, yet I am ready to embrace life.

*I allow my soul to be set free and am no longer
an abuser's wife.*

I stand firmly in my shoes as I run toward my destiny.

*I have been praying, believing and achieving,
knowing I have finally found me.*

I am a woman of beauty who was in search of her crown.

*It's the foundation of my worthiness
that had been buried underground.*

I owe it all to my heavenly father whom watches from above,

*Leading, guiding, and shielding me
as I learn the meaning of self-love.*

I am now a strong woman with the strength of many men.

*I have knocked down the walls of my shame, and rest my pain
in my father's hands.*

I am a like iron soldier determined to protect my crown.

It's been missing for a lifetime, and it needed to be found.

As a daughter grows up without a father, she grows up unaware of her crown. This crown validates and defines her womanhood, her identity, and her worth. When she has additional trauma in her childhood, she becomes emotionally stuck at whatever age she felt secure. Because of the emotional immaturity, she becomes emotionally contaminated, and no matter how deep this infection was buried, it finds a way to show itself even when she isn't aware of it. The only way to break the cycle is by finding her validation and self-love. Once I was able to recognize I was a woman without a '*crown*', I was ready to search for it. How can I heal from my past, validate my self-worth, and create my new story?

There I was searching for my crown: my self-worth and self-validation. I realized I would never get it from my daddy, so I had to figure out how to give it to myself. I knew this was going to be intense, because I was about to face myself. In order to find emotional healing, I needed to face all the things that wounded me. I had to brace myself for this long journey of self-discovery. I trusted God and went with it, because I truly desired the healing. I had to commit to my emotional well-being, and a life investment in self-love. Because my life was in such a mess, I found myself overwhelmed with emotions, and I took a timeout to sit alone with me and do my work.

When I started my journey, I had no visual roadmap. My mornings were spent on long walks with just God and me. I spoke to him, walked, prayed, and cried in search of direction. I knew he was with me because he began to speak to my soul as he guided me through my journey. I stayed spiritually connected and allowed God to lead from one step to the next. In the middle of the night, he would awaken me as he whispered the next set of instructions. I recorded everything: every experience, every prayer, every thought, and every answer, etc. At the end of my journey, I had written these steps to healing.

1. Remove the mask

As a child I learned how to bury pain, and I had constructed a mask to hide my wounds from the world. Before I could do anything else, I had to remove the mask, the outer shell I showed to the world. It protected me, and hid my raw emotions. However, it was those superficial layers keeping me in bondage. I tried to be anything that defined me on the surface—the professional woman, nice lady, boys' mom, etc., but was afraid to face who I was underneath. It was easier to remain hidden, because anything beyond the surface was far too painful to acknowledge.

Taking the mask off wasn't easy, but I had to face the core essence so I could discover the root of my pain. After you wear a mask so long, you begin to believe it is your truth. However, the real truth was that the little abandoned Sonja was causing emotional mishap, and she was about to expose me. The best thing for me to do was face myself before she told any more of my secrets.

I spent time in the mirror getting acquainted with myself so I could face the mess underneath the layers. This was one of the hardest things to do. At first I was afraid to face her, because I wasn't sure I would be able to handle all of the pain she had endured. I knew I needed to stop running from my childhood abandonment, shame, and disappointments. I needed to accept who I was, so I could rewrite my own story.

As I was able to face myself, I begin to ask myself the questions I never had the courage to ask before.

- How did you get to be so broken?
- Why do you keep allowing yourself to be victimized?
- Why do you keep attaching yourself to men who abuse and/or abandon you?
- Where did you put your self-worth?
- Have you ever really loved yourself?

These were some of the toughest questions, but I had to face them. I asked God to give me the courage and wisdom to find the answers. They were hard to accept, but I knew I needed to come clean if I wanted to be delivered—especially considering

I was the one who helped others fix themselves. Wow! I was a therapist admitting to myself I also had things I needed to fix. Once I removed my mask and acknowledged my truth, I moved onto the process.

2. Get it all out

Once the mask was off, I begin to make a list of things I knew I needed to change about myself. This was a very important list, because it was my working document. I begin to ask myself a series of new questions:

- What makes you do what you do?
- What is your first memory of hurt, and how did it affect you?
- What led you on your self-destructive cycle?

I had to find out *where the hurt* was before I allowed myself to move from this spot.

I relied on my faith when I felt weak so I could get up and start again. I had to go cold turkey, and give up my artificial soothers which were affirmation from others, self-sacrifice, and avoidance. They only offered a temporary fix. When I came down off my emotional high, I had to face the hurt that was still within me. I realized they felt good at the time, but removing them would mean experiencing the feelings in the raw.

I was afraid of the experience, but it was time to stop running away from my past, and do the repairs. I couldn't worry about the people I would disappoint; they had already turned against me. When I realized how much of a doormat I had allowed myself to be, I felt foolish. However, I realized I was loving in a broken heart. At many moments, I felt like I needed to cry, scream, and yell. I found myself needing to escape from my busy life so I could come to this place and write about my pain. I allowed myself to have some private time to release my thoughts, because there were times when they came as an intrusion on my happiness. I couldn't do anything with all of the painful memories other than face them. It was time to release the pain I had buried so deep.

As I released it, I wrote about it. I wrote about the missing things, the lost love, the hurt and abuse, and the relationship I had wanted with my father. I wrote a letter to God telling him about the healing I needed from him. While I was in this process, I often found myself bursting into tears in a middle of a smile. I had held back these emotions for so long, once I opened the door, they were waiting to escape. Every time I released a part of my story on paper, I felt a large piece of the heavy stone being removed from my feet, as if I had been shackled.

3. Go back and rescue her

I had to take an emotional road trip back through the beginning of my life. I needed to go and visit the little girl who was hurting inside of me. I had to get to know her, and spend time on a journey of discovery so I could figure out what had happened to her. I realized I needed to tend to her wounds so I could restore her innocence, and help her heal. It was time to stop loving through her, because she does not know how to keep my heart out of trouble. I had to heal her so she could grow into the woman I needed to be.

I had a lot of work to do. I wasn't sure where I needed to start, but I knew it was time to do some self-discovery. I spent a lot of time with her, stopping in at every phase of her life. I got off on every stop so I could discover what healing was needed, and I mourned for her so I could free her. Every time I finished grieving at one stop, I got up and kept moving so I could get started again. I reached many low points as I witnessed her pain, and at one point, I could not go through it any more. However, I realized after taking a long break, God was not going to let me rest until I completed this healing. After all, I had asked for it.

When I got really weak, I would recite one of my favorite scriptures, and God became my source of strength. "Yay though I walk through the valley of the shadow of death, I will fear no evil for God is with me. " The Lord was my shepherd and I had to remind myself that what happened to her in childhood does not make me into the woman I am today. It is only a part of who I was, but does not have to define me. I knew once I started opening up some of those memories, my heart would be overloaded with emotions. I did not want to face this pain, yet I knew I wanted to heal. I had to step back and close many doors before I could reenter them.

I went back to the little three-year-old girl who was afraid when her daddy was abusing her mommy, the seven-year-old who lost her mom to mental illness, the eight, twelve, fourteen, sixteen and eighteen-year-old who was sexually abused, and the girl who grew up without a father. I had to hold all of them and comfort them so they knew they were now okay. While on this part of the journey, I cried and cried for her. I had held onto so many tears, sometimes the mere fact of letting them out brought a great amount of peace.

4. Let her know you love her

Being totally honest was admitting I didn't know how *to love myself.* Before I could love myself as a woman, I had to love the abandoned little girl who hid inside of me, holding her battered heart. I had to stop waiting for my unavailable daddy to validate her, and had to figure out how to validate her through my own love. I grew up feeling alone and ashamed because I did not know how to love myself. I remember a time where my order of love was not in sync. I was in love with pleasing whoever threatened to leave me. I constantly gave up what I owed to God, and carried the dead weight of pleasing others. It was time to stop creating a false sense of love, and find out how to discover true self-love.

I began to write love letters to the little girl who needed to know she was loved. I wanted her to know all of the wonderful things I discovered about her while I was on my visit. While journaling, I began to make a list of the many unique gifts and talents I had rediscovered about young Sonja—things that had gone unacknowledged. Sonja was a good singer, a good artist, a writer, very smart, and even a good dancer. She was also kind, sweet, beautiful, and loving. Every day I challenged myself to come up with at least two things I loved about myself. If I struggled to think of something on my own, I would ask someone who I knew really loved me. This became a ritual, and every day I was feeding myself validations.

I turned my list into a love letter to myself, and typed it on my favorite color of paper. I posted it on my mirror as a daily reminder of my promise to love myself first. As time went on, I was becoming more confident, and knew I was worthy of love and validation. When I sent this energy out into the universe, it followed me. I stopped searching for love to define me, and I defined the love for which I searched.

People began to value my worth by what I showed them. When I showed I was worth gold, they would treat me as such. Now feeling so much love from within, it satisfies the longing left by my father. I know God loves me, and has created me as I am, and because I have found my center, nothing can shake that. I no longer allow anyone to place a value on my self-worth and/or accomplishments, especially those I know don't love me. Only God defines who I am, and I seek after his approval. God loved me so much he did not let me stay stuck. He allowed me to go through this until I was ready to deal with it—and let it go. I now realize love should come in this order: God, yourself, and others.

5. Embrace all of who you are

I had to embrace all of what I had discovered about my pain. As I faced the reality of my life, I asked God to help me understand the purpose of it. Once I embraced my truth, I began to release, grow, and heal. Embracing what was broken in me, allowed me to gain the courage to repair it. As I faced the root of my shame, I accepted it, and let it go because it could no longer hold me captive. All my secrets were revealed, and I was no longer carrying the dead weight.

As I continued to work on myself, I accepted the things I didn't like. Every time I discovered something new, I prayed for the courage to accept it so it too could be released. One of the hardest things I had to do was to admit to myself I was a liar. I would rather lie to someone about my true feelings than stand up to them when I knew they were taking advantage of me. I pretended I wasn't aware of it, and would smile back in their faces while a hole was burning in my heart. I lied and convinced myself God made me strong enough to take a beating, and I stuck with it. I shut up, took it, believed it, buried it, and lived secretly in the abuse. This was a lie and an excuse to cover up my most terrifying fear, which was to come face to face with conflict. Guess what, God was good to me, but he did not make me with an iron heart, and did not create me for the purpose of taking pain. The truth was I deserved to be loved, and God created me to be a loving person. Today I am able to receive love freely, and give love away unconditionally.

6. Share her story

God gave me the courage to face people upfront by asking this simple question: Do you want all of me, or bits in pieces? If you desire all of me, allow me to give myself to you as a whole being. This meant they had to accept what was wounded, battered, and broken. I was ready to let go of the secrets, and I needed those around me to understand my truth. I had always been very private and secretive about my extended family and childhood experiences. As an adult, I continued to lie about shameful experiences when my life had been in danger. At times, I lived in fear of exposure, and made myself distant from close friends. No one around me knew anything about my childhood, absent father, mentally ill mother, or sexual abuse.

Yet I was burdened by the hidden secrets, and I kept telling lies to keep them concealed. Once I began to share my truth, I begin to find so much peace. In the beginning, I found it hard to recite my story because it was hard to make sense of all of the tragic memories. However, as I began peeling back one layer at a time, many of my closest friends were shocked by my truth, because they had assumed I had grown up in a normal, intact family.

When I told one of my best friends my truth, before I could expose it all, she burst into tears. Her tears caught me off guard, and I found myself embracing her. When I asked her why she was so upset, she said she couldn't imagine me going through those things. She was the first person to whom I had revealed myself, and I said, "Thanks, Tonyia, for feeling my pain. I will never forget how you cried for me." As time went on, I began to share when I felt it was appropriate, including public speaking engagements. Today I feel totally set free—I am no longer ashamed of anything that I have experienced over my lifetime.

7. Beware of your destructive emotional cycle

I needed to figure out what kept me connected to the little girl who was in pain. She was timid, weak, and fearful of rejection. I would often allow her to be in control of my emotions as I subconsciously attached myself to abusive relationships, ones which kept her wounded. Because I was living through her pain, I allowed myself to be seduced by men who were familiar to her. She was trying to undo the abandonment holding her captive. While I was seeking a mate, she was longing to win her father's love, and what was broken in her, drew me to men who were like her father. She was convinced if I repaired them, they would in return repair her broken heart.

I had to heal her so I could stop her from sacrificing me. I could not keep operating in this destructive cycle that kept me emotionally bankrupt. It was time to stop letting people withdraw from my emotional bank without making a deposit. I was giving out unearned emotional paychecks, and in turn, my heart was left in a million pieces. It needed to be mended before I could move on to any other relationships.

When I stopped trying to find love through the abandoned little girl inside of me, I was able align myself with people who desire healthy relationships. I began to take control, and I changed my cycle. In many cases, it meant letting go of people who tried to keep the little girl inside of me in captivity. They were used to responding to her, and unwilling to accept when I presented myself to them as a strong woman. I was ready to let go, and let them come to their own conclusion and self-discovery.

8. Encourage yourself to get through it

You have to find some way to encourage yourself. People may not readily be available to catch your tears. Some days it felt like it was only God and me, even when I had many people to whom I could have reached out. However, when I was in the trenches, I knew no one had the power to get me through, but God himself. When I felt overwhelmed, I had to encourage myself, and speak my breakthrough into existence. Despite how tough it seemed, I continued to love myself. I believed in my deliverance, even when Satan wanted me to believe it was impossible.

My grandma's impression on my life

I have to thank my grandma for being a praying woman. She taught me how to pray and believe in miracles. I believe her prayers kept me, when I could not keep myself. I knew God was all in this, and I was going to overcome this because I believed. I knew my discovery was my process, and I was worthy to be loved because I belong to God. Change takes time, and a lot of courage. I relied on God for my deliverance. I went on many spiritual retreats where it was only God, me, and my tears. My soothing came from praise and worship music, and on the dark days, I overindulged in it as an effort to bring joy back into my soul. I didn't let myself stay down too long because I didn't want to get stuck. Even in my sadness, I let God know I was worshiping him.

If I was in my car, at work, or in my bedroom, when I needed spiritual healing, I pulled out my spiritual medicine, and I would revive my weakened soul. If I couldn't get to my music, I relied on a scripture to get me through. "No weapon formed against me shall prosper," Isaiah 54.17. "For God so loved the world that he gave his only begotten son so that who so ever believes in him shall not perish but have ever lasting life." (English Standard Version, John 3.16).

Even when I grew distant from God, I knew I had a calling on my life. He has forgiven me even when I fell out of faith. He was there with his arms open, waiting for my return. I would never be gone too long, because God would snatch me back. He knew exactly when to do it, right when I needed him the most.

9. Let the healing begin

In order to heal completely, I had to tear down my old foundation built on lies and deceptions, and reconstruct my truth. It was time to learn how to stay in peace and rebuild a foundation of love, truth, and worthiness. I sat alone and did the repairs so the damage would stop presenting itself in my life. It was a matter of reprogramming, rebooting, and reliving. When I found myself, I knew who I was, and who I wanted to bring into my life. I knew God would not allow me to open my heart to anyone who is not worthy of it. Because I wanted it, I believed in it, worked on it, and waited for it, I took time out to heal the emotional scars before entering into any other relationship. I wanted to tend to every wound so they were properly mended.

The day I realized I had a voice was the day everything changed. I started to set boundaries and expectations of how I wanted others to treat me, and I let people know when they hurt or offended me. This was huge, because before now, I never allowed myself to have a voice. I stopped attaching to people who responded to the broken little girl, and sought out people who welcomed the strong woman. I was no longer seeing myself as victimized and abandoned. My healing was happening *right on time.*

At times, I came close to giving up, but God gave me the courage to hang in there, and wait on my breakthrough. I was in a place of stillness where God kept me from myself until I was ready to deal with myself. If I would have reacted out of my own consciousness, with all I have gone through, I could have lost my mind. Because I trusted in him and hung in there, the chains began to break from my feet. The bondage could no longer contain me. As I discovered my healing points, I found my center and emotional peace. Here I am, the woman God intended me to be.

10. Let the transformation begin

Sometimes we heal our wounds, but we still hold on to some

of the baggage because of the comfort. I found the peace within my faith, and I rose above the things which have traumatized me. During this phase of healing, I attended a support group for women dealing with domestic violence. I quickly realized this group was not appropriate for me because I had healed from those events. I did not need to be in a place where I had to try to connect to their pain in order to fit in. I no longer viewed myself as a victim, and sometimes I suppressed my victory in fear of boasting in front of women who were still wounded. After attending for several weeks, I was done. However, when appropriate, there is nothing wrong with attending a support group because it can be beneficial for many victims. I am proud of the courage God has given me as he mended me. I refuse to carry the shame of my mistakes while others live free of guilt. I know Christ is a healer, and through him I have been restored.

As I live in truth, and the mere fact I let it all go, brings great peace. It feels good to live outside my mask. I accept the emotional absence of my earthly father, yet my heavenly father provides. No more rewind buttons, it is time to press play and go forward. Whew! Thank you, Jesus! Give me the strength to keep reexamining my life to assure it remains intact. Some people I love refuse to accept my transformation because they had become accustomed to misusing me. Many of them exited rather quickly, while others will continue to try to force me back into my broken heart.

I am now assured the cycle has been broken as I give myself permission to love freely. Today I stand strong because I am a woman who can now understand my pain. The memories come every now and again. As a child, I buried them; as a woman, I faced facing them. My relationship with God became my driving force, and the chains kept breaking. I realize healing is a process, and I am almost free. I can feel it, smell, and see it, so I will continue to breathe it into existence. Now I had found my crown, and I am ready to prepare for my crowning. However, another part of the healing process is *forgiveness*. Because I wanted to be free, I had to forgive those who I allowed to harm me.

In the next chapter, I will walk you through my steps leading to forgiveness.

CHAPTER 10:

How Does She Forgive Him, and Them?

Dear Heavenly Father,

Help me to release the negative offenses that harmed me. Restore my broken heart by mending wounds. Give me the courage to face my offender, and help me to break the chains given unto me. Allow me to move forward and regain control over my destiny, purpose, and being. Amen

In the previous chapter, the journey toward healing was focused on acknowledging and understanding the hurt. Once the hurt has been acknowledged, we are able to move toward forgiveness and let go of everything that has harmed us. Forgiveness is an action done through a process, and it is not something you can subscribe. Many of us believe if we say we forgive someone, all of the hurt, sadness, and disappointment will simply go away. However, we find ourselves confused when we realize what we wanted to release, still holds us captive.

I share my own journey of forgiveness and pray as you walk through this with me, you will also be able to come to a place of freedom and forgiveness. You may not think this chapter is relevant to your life as many believers think they have already forgiven, let go, and moved on. However, I ask that you stay with me and read the entire chapter before making that call.

Many of us go through life unaware that we are holding on to grudges, resentment, and old hurts. We allow the wounds of our past to guide our decisions and drive our relationships, and oftentimes, we are distrustful, guarded, and unhealthy. Some of us are aware of our lack of forgiveness while others live in denial. What we don't realize is *our inability to forgive keeps us hostage.* For years I fooled myself into believing I held no hurt, fostered no anger, and felt no pain in regards to my past. However, if the truth were told, there were so many people I needed to forgive. It was one thing to admit to being hurt, but the act of forgiving those that had hurt me meant going to another whole level of healing…and living.

We never think about forgiveness being our responsibility or that it is a large part of our healing process. I asked God to show me what I needed to do so I could learn to forgive. I didn't want to just say it. I wanted to live in forgiveness!!! And to do this, I needed my broken heart to be bathed in it. The only forgiveness I had ever learned about was the forgiveness that Christ poured out upon us. How do I get to a place of being able to pour that kind of forgiveness out upon others? Growing up I was told I needed to forgive and forget. However, I never really learned about forgiveness. What I had learned was avoidance. In fact, it wasn't uncommon for someone to feel hurt by another family member, and not speak to them for a long period of time, even though we are a Christian family. They learn to bury their pain, and avoid the person altogether. We then used our faith to cover up pain and I will be the first to admit it.

I also learned very early, as a Christian, you weren't allowed to be broken, and I learned to mask the pain. I grew up hearing sayings like, "Forgive and forget," "Let go and let God," "Turn the other cheek," "Don't worry, let them reap what they sowed," and "Don't let the sun go down on your wrath." Although I believe in the word of God, I think many of us Christians misuse or misunderstand the true meaning of forgiveness. I believe God wants us to go through the whole process of healing so that we can receive the gift of forgiveness.

While on this road of forgiveness, I asked God to show me where to start. I soon realized the one person who had harmed me the most was myself. I was on the verge of hating myself before God tapped me on the shoulder, spread his arms for me, and said "Enough." He showed me I needed to forgive myself before I could forgive anyone else. What? How in the world was I going to it? Whoever thinks about forgiving themselves? Not me! However, I had spent a lifetime secretly blaming myself for many things. I was ready to forgive others, but I didn't know I had to forgive myself, too.

I had been so angry with myself because my gullible spirit, and desire to be loved, had misled me into many broken relationships. When each one of the men walked away, I was losing another piece of my already-shattered heart. I pretended to smile and reframed my mask, moving on becoming more fragile, until I would eventually break altogether. The more mistakes I made, the more the shame and guilt piled up. I was holding more things against myself than anyone else.

Forgiving myself

- *I forgive myself for losing my pride, financial status, stability, and many dreams because I kept falling victim to the toxic relationships.*
- *I forgive myself for being broken and emotionally battered as I ended one relationship after the other feeling unwanted, stupid, and shameful.*
- *I forgive myself for allowing myself to be depleted, and for believing if I gave enough, love enough, worked hard enough, they would finally love me.*
- *I forgive myself for loving blindly, and for loving in my pain. I forgive myself for hiding the physical, emotional, verbal, sexual, and financial abuse in an effort to protect others.*
- *I forgive myself for putting my self-worth in someone else's hands, and for sacrificing everything because I had convinced myself I was not worthy a voice.*
- *I forgive myself for sacrificing myself, believing it was my only way of survival.*
- *I forgive myself for not knowing how to love myself enough to know how I deserved to be loved.*

Self-forgiveness was difficult but God opened my eyes and helped me to understand what had driven me. I now knew why I had become *that woman*. It wasn't because I didn't desire to be in a loving relationship, but I was stuck. God began to show me myself as the broken little girl, and I begin to feel an overwhelming presence of him around me. I kept seeing the image of his precious son stretched out on the cross before me, and I knew he had forgiven me. Soon I begin to realize it was time to let go of the secret resentment I held against myself. I begin to see myself the way I had seen others, and I realized I had only become what I had experienced.

As a result of my abandonment and childhood trauma, I learned to seek love in desperation. I desperately wanted to be loved, and was willing to sacrifice myself for it. I grew up chasing after the feeling of abandonment left by my father, trying to appease the pain remaining from my sexual abuse, and the need to please, driven by my longing to be loved. With this came clarity, and I knew I was worthy of my own forgiveness. Today I proclaim I have been exonerated, and these sins have been removed from me. I am free of the false accusations I brought against myself, and today my journey has become my choice.

Forgiving my father

I had forgiven myself, and it was time for me to move down the road of forgiveness. Before I could forgive the others who I allowed to leave me broken as a woman, I realized I had to go to the root where my heart was first broken. The first man who ever broke my heart was my father. The pain from this experience created a foundation of brokenness I framed my heart around. I did not realize until the day of my phone conversation with my father, I still held years of hurt, desperation, and shame because he repeatedly abandoned me. I realized I had to understand why I needed to forgive him.

My father was emotionally and physically absent from my life until I was in my late twenties. With the exception of the codependent relationship with my father while he was in prison, he and I had little long-term interaction. I never felt like he was there for me, as much as I felt obligated to be there for him. When he was released from prison, he had no real interest in being my emotional daddy, despite all the years I had invested in him. We established a superficial relationship created around a vicious cycle of abandonment. Our relationship appeared good as long as things remained on the surface. However, if a situation caused the surface to be scratched, he would bail on me, leaving me with the same feelings of abandonment I had felt when I was a child.

There was a wave of emotions I never got to put anywhere, so I buried them. I never had the courage to ask about his past. I secretly resented my father, because when he did appear to be compassionate enough to help, he had a way of throwing whatever he did for me in my face, and this would cancel any of his acts of kindness.

Although I would be hurt, I sucked it up, withdrew, and waited for another opportunity to jump into his arms. I pretended I didn't need him while I still secretly longed for his love, guidance, and approval. I was angry because I desperately wanted to learn something from him. When I reached out to him, hoping he would scoop me up in his arms and hold me there, I felt rejection. I badly needed to feel his arms around me as he whispered comforting words in my ears. For a brief moment, I hated him for being so narrow-minded and self-absorbed. I wanted to scream so he could hear my pain, but I remained silent.

I realized I needed to forgive my father for all the pain caused by him. I had to go back and find healing within our broken relationship so I could move forward. Although I haven't spoken to my father since, I have written him a letter of forgiveness. He needed to hear about the hurt I carried, I realized he had only learned to love in his own brokenness. Perhaps he carried the wounds of his own difficult childhood, and some pain in his life prevented him from being the father I needed him to be. Maybe he doesn't interact with his daughters because his connection to us reminds him of the man he had been in the past. Some people simply aren't strong enough to face all of who they were.

Today I can forgive him and pray this healing between us becomes complete. I believe my father loves me on the surface, but I am not sure if he knows how to love me beyond it. I don't believe he knows how to be a father to the adult children he has left broken. It is easier for my father to view my relationship disasters as my failures, but I hope he understands how not having him there to guide me had everything to do with my brokenness.

If I could ask God for one thing, it would be to touch my father's heart, help him realize what was broken in him, how it affected his children, and understand the meaning of a father's love. I know I am now an adult, but he can do so much more with his daughters.

I forgive him for not being there for my children. However, I can't erase the resent they have towards him because they want a grandpa to love them, be a positive role model, and teach them about manhood. I know he is capable of teaching them because he is being a wonderful father to my stepsister and stepbrother, and an awesome grandfather to his step grandchildren. I am praying one day he is able to offer the same to his own grandchildren because they also deserve the best of him.

The final phase of forgiveness

The final phase of forgiveness came a little easier than I thought it would be. I was very angry at the last guy who had hurt me. I spit fire at him, and made him pay for all the anger I had harbored over my lifetime. Although he was actually the one who had treated me the best, he got all of my rage, because he was the one who awakened my pain. The two prior relationships left me emotionally, physically, and financially abused, but never angry. I think I was angrier with him because he was a born-again Christian. Despite the obvious, I expected him to be like Christ. He promised to never hurt me, and I allowed myself to be forced me into a marriage for which I wasn't ready for.

However, because I was broken, I obligated myself into being a devoted wife to him, even when I was beginning to realize I needed to be by myself. My gut feelings were against it, but I allowed Satan to deceive me, and I fell into the trap. When the ceiling collapsed on the marriage, I was faced with more deception. In the beginning, I was angry and threw all the blame on him, but soon I started to realize it really wasn't about him at all. The unresolved hurt toward my father had been carried on to the men who I allowed to abuse me. I had written myself off as a victim long ago because it was easier than to face conflict and possibility of abandonment. When I began to accept responsibility, and acknowledge they had only done what I had allowed they to do, forgiveness came easily.

In addition to my father and my "exes", I realized I had been carrying hurt from the many friends, family members, etc., who I had allowed to wound my heart. I was secretly carrying resentment when many of these people were not even aware they had hurt me. While on my journey of forgiving, I wanted to let go of everything negatively attached to my spirit. Growing up, I was told if someone wrongs you, you should let go and let God or turn the other cheek. As a woman, I realized that I needed to go to him or her, tell him how he offended you, and give them the opportunity to correct it.

I collected a list of people I needed to forgive, the men I allowed to victimize me, a few of my family members and close friends, and of course, my father. I like to call this my list of redemption. If I was still holding onto something a person had done to harm me, it went on this list. I put them in order of priority by the value of the relationship, and wrote down each offense, and how I felt about it. Before I knew it, I had written each of them a letter telling my version of the story. Many of the letters were never received because I burned them as a way of releasing everything that I had been holding on too. However, a few needed to be mailed. I purchased the most beautiful blank stationary I could find, and I begin to write their letters. I wasn't looking to reestablish the relationship, but I was ready to release the unhealthy emotional connection for which I was responsible. If a new beginning presented itself, I was open to it as well. Regardless of the outcome, these were letters I needed to write so I could close those chapters of my life, and move forward.

Once I begin to let it all go, I no longer resented any of them, and I was no longer carrying the hurt from anyone in my heart. Holding onto negative emotions affects a person's mental and physical well-being. My body had been weighed down by hatred, anger, and stress while others lived on in their happiness. I realized it was my responsibility to set standards because people accepted only what I had presented to them. If you accept mistreatment, you will be mistreated, but if you expect good treatment, people will treat you well.

Finally, I felt free. I felt lighter and more connected to my life and my faith. Later in the book I will talk more about setting relationships standards. Below is a roadmap to forgiveness. If you feel you want to reach out to someone you need to forgive, these steps may be helpful, even to open an opportunity for conversation. Perhaps you may want to write a letter, and then burn it. Whatever you choose to do, it is up to you.

Steps to forgiveness

1. Acknowledge the pain, and let it present itself. Most often we let other feelings handle what has harmed us. Don't be afraid to expose the buried hurt, and let the tears flow if you need to. I'm not saying to go the other person crying like a baby. Perhaps before you approach them, get it out.

2. Make sure you have an understanding so you know how you are affected. Explain to them how you have carried this offense to other aspects of your life, and the effects of burying and avoidance. If you don't know how or why you were affected, you should spend some time exploring your feelings beforehand.

3. Tell your story from your point of view. It doesn't matter what Aunt Sue says he did. It matters you know what he did, and how you feel about it. When you tell your story from someone else's point of view, it's not coming from real emotions.

4. You have to be willing to listen to their response, and accept it, even if the response is not what you expected to hear. Give them an opportunity to process what you say, and understand your point of view. They may not be able to acknowledge your story, now or ever.

5. Accept who they are in their own brokenness, and know they may have used it as an excuse to offend others. Some people will remain stuck and no one but God can unglue them. It may be too painful for them to look at the pain they have caused you because it reminds them of the pain they received from someone else.

6. Accept what you have lost, the hurt you incurred, and forgive them. Don't base your forgiveness on their full admission. Don't expect an immediate apology or their understanding. Many people don't want to hear what they have done to you, because they have not done enough soul searching to realize who they are. They may not acknowledge their faults or any part of your story. Move on from them. Realize this person may be broken. The only power they have is the power we give to them. They become powerful if you allow their offenses against you to control your life. When you base your forgiveness on your freedom, they become immediately powerless.

As I mentioned earlier, forgiveness does not come easy. Sometimes we get caught up in holding onto unforgiveness, and we can't move forward. If we don't forgive, we keep our own sins attached to us, and they become blessing blockers. I had to go through these steps a few times before I was able to actually process all of the steps of forgiveness. Through the process, I had to be totally honest with myself so I could figure out what was causing me to hold this baggage and the inability to forgive. Truth be told, sometimes we benefit from holding on to pain. For example, if we focus on what was done to us, we use it as our excuse for not trusting others. It was tough to accept, but it was the truth. I needed to let it go because it was no longer my pain to hold.

I realized I cannot truly love again until I processed through this final stage of healing. I found myself going on many spiritual retreats to break through this final piece of emotional bondage. As long as we are human, we will continue to have setbacks. However, we do not have to remain stuck. When I found myself in a setback, I acknowledged it, gave myself permission to let it go, and relied on my faith to push through it. I knew I could not obtain total deliverance until I was able to fully forgive.

Once I was able to understand the true meaning of forgiveness, I was free. However, I realized I had to be aware of behaviors that could cause me to hold on to things I wanted to release. I had to be mindful of relationships that could keep me in bondage. For those mendable relationships, I reminded myself to keep my voice present. There were many relationships, which I needed to let go. It didn't mean I did not forgive them; it meant we are at a different place, and I needed to allow them the opportunity to go through their own healing process. Some people were not ready to accept the fact they had offended me, and were clueless about what I needed from them. For example: my father never responded to my letter, and he has not spoken to me in over three years. I accept where he is at, and the only thing I could do was pray for him. It is now up to me to set the standards for the relationships I enter.

As I move through this journey of forgiveness, I was able to leave all of the pain, anger, sadness, hopeless, fear, disappointments, and whatever negative feelings that I held from the past. This process took a little over a year, but it was the most productive year of my entire life. I recall the day I fell to my knees asking God to help me through those painful moments. I had no idea where he was taking me.

I still wake up with the feelings of joy and peace because I have learned the meaning of forgiveness. Sometimes I feel overwhelmed because I feel the spirit of God all around me. Today I can honestly say I am free. I acknowledge my survival, and I will never allow myself to carry the weight of unforgiveness. I am powerful because I am in control of my destiny and my purpose in life.

CHAPTER 11:

She Crowns Herself Queen

When you can wake up every morning believing you are worthy of everything that belongs to you, this is when you become Queen. Every woman deserves happiness, success, love, respect, and the freedom to be who she desires to be.

She Crowns Herself Queen

One day I work up, looked in the mirror, and realized I had finally become whole—I discovered my self-worth. I live in my healing, I am always conscious of unhealthy emotional patterns that can connect to my past cycle. I'm not saying I won't go back and restore some of those old relationships I lost along the way. However, as I continued to perfect my emotional growth and understand what I desire, I gave myself permission to enjoy my own existence. Sometimes I allow myself to miss birthday parties, graduations, special events, etc. It wasn't because I don't want to celebrate and enjoy my family and friends. I needed to allow myself the freedom to do what was best for me.

Today I listen to my body, mind, and spirit. If I fell tired, I give myself permission to be tired. In the past, I would force myself to do things for people, even when I knew it was almost impossible, and when I failed, it was thrown in my face. In the beginning of my transformation, I struggled with the guilt. However, I did not stay down for long, because God quickly came in and replaced it with peace. Some never understood my need to care for myself because this journey was not about them as much as it was about me. For long periods of isolation, I spent time writing, praying, reading, etc. At times, I offended people close to my heart because they did not understand the work for which God was preparing me to do. They were familiar with the old Sonja replying to their beck and call. However, I stayed focused, found my peace, and surrendered to my purpose.

God patiently waited until I was ready to be delivered before he grabbed me. As mentioned in an earlier chapter, he even allowed a perfect stranger to speak about my purpose without even knowing my name or anything about me. She knew many women were waiting for me to finish this book so they could be healed because of my testimony. Wow!

I pray I am reaching you. As in the previous chapters, I recorded various steps as I went through my journey. Next are the steps I recorded as I learned to validate, love, and establish my self-worth.

I hope when you walk through these steps, you too will be able to follow the roadmap to crowning yourself Queen.

1. Get in touch with your spirituality.

People have many different spiritual beliefs, so I am not going to debate religions. However, I knew I had to connect to something bigger than me because I needed my faith back. Because I am a Christian, I know what it means to believe in Jesus Christ. I grew up in the church, and at times, I was deeply committed to my faith. However, because of my brokenness, and my longing for my daddy's love, it was easy for a non-believing man to come along and knock me off my path. At times, I would try to fight for my faith, but eventually I would be overcome by the fear of being emotionally harmed and/or abandoned. Sometimes I would secretly worship, but I was never able to fully commit.

It was so amazing how God was so patient with me. It was through his forgiveness I was able to forgive myself, my fathers, and others. There were days when I felt overwhelmed by his presence. The closer I got to him, the more he revealed to me. When I say everything became clear, I mean crystal clear. I know Christ is a healer, and through him I was restored on so many levels. I couldn't be here today if my faith had not been my driving force. God truly chases after those he loves.

2. Find out who you are, and where you belong in the world.

Before I could connect with anyone, I needed to connect with myself. I needed to find out who I was, and what I like to do, how I wanted others to treat me, and what I wanted the world to know about me. I took time to find my voice, and used it to empower my happiness. In my life I had been defined as someone's woman, mother, sister, victim, property, etc. However, I needed to know my own definition of me as my own woman. God has a purpose for us all, and it is time for me to live up to my purpose. After years of constantly giving to others, now it is time to give to myself, and affirm my rights to take care of me.

I began to set standards and to live in the life I have created for myself. I finally felt worthy enough to be around people who have established themselves, and had the same standards. For once, I was able to do things that made me happy. I realized I had a very silly side of me, and liked to make people laugh. For me, laughter helped maintain my happiness. I try to find at least two or three reasons to laugh each day, and I usually am thinking of a funny joke to keep myself amused. Sometimes I find myself cracking up even when I know people around me may think I'm crazy. However, they have no idea how much joy I have. The more transparent I become, the more I began to find my peace. I want to scream, "What peace, what joy, what love!" The sound of this soothes my spirit.

3. Believe that you are a Queen, and wear the crown.

Every woman deserves to be her own Queen, and proclaim her self-worth. I began to accept all of my beauty as a woman, and walk in confidence in it. I remember when I first started transforming. So many people would be drawn to my spirit. Strangers walked up to me, and said I had a beautiful presence, I was stunning, I was glowing, and something about me compelled them to speak to me. At first, I didn't understand, and felt very strange. Then to realize what was going on. It was like God preparing me for my worthiness as I was transforming. Even today, when I go into a room of unfamiliar people, people still walk up to me, acknowledging my inner beauty. It humbles me, because I remember a time when it was hidden behind a mask. I am not arrogant, but I walk proudly in my self-worth as I drew people to me who accepted my validation of myself.

I realize the more comfortable I grew in my crown, the more power I had over how people treated me. I knew I could never give anyone the power to remove it, and I no longer look to people for validation. I stand my ground by not letting anyone adjust my standards. If someone is not okay with who I have become, I am willing to set them free.

4. Find out how to fall in love with yourself.

It is a wonderful feeling to be able to look in the mirror and say, "I am so in love with me, all of me!" I could never really love anyone until I loved myself. Before I allowed myself to fall in love with anyone else, I needed to take the time and fall in love with me. You should never love anyone more than you love yourself. I remember a time when I put others before God and myself. I constantly gave up what I owed to God and myself, in an effort to appease others so they would not abandoned me.

I acknowledge the greatness within me, and accepted I am a child of God. I owed it to myself to seek out what I loved, needed, and wanted. I started to pamper myself by going on dates by myself, taking vacations, doing makeovers, etc. I sometimes still look in the mirror to remind myself of my beauty, because I truly love looking inside of me. I embrace who I have become, and set standards of love within my close circle of family and friends. I no longer love in a broken heart because I know what true love really is.

5. Invest in your personal growth to keep your self-esteem lifted.

I created a bucket list of activities I have wanted to do. At the beginning of each month, I wrote down an activity and a list of steps wanted to complete. Starting and finishing something new gives you a sense of accomplishment. I started working out, going on bike rides, writing my book, and singing in the choir again. I also started public speaking, and discovered I enjoy doing it. I am beginning a new journey as an author, public speaker, and presenter. I am looking forward to doing seminars to help women walk through the steps in this book. Recently I decided to begin my PHD in marriage and family therapy so I can further my research. This was something I always dreamed of doing, but never had before the courage.

These were some of the things I had on my bucket list. You can create a bucket list many different ways. Perhaps someone may want to finish a degree, learn to sew, learn to swim, go to cooking class, quit smoking, change your habits, finish a big project, etc. I think you get my drift. If nothing else, I made a promise to make every effort to present myself as my best every morning, even if I don't have anywhere special to go.

6. Make sure people in your close circle know how to treat you.

Many people are afraid to discuss their expectations within a friendship. I realized I had to let people know how I needed to be treated, and let them know what I was willing to give. I no longer wanted to surround myself with people who had malicious intent. It didn't matter if they were a sibling or close friend. From that day forward, I wanted only people in my close circle who I knew had my back. If they hurt me in the past, I may have forgiven them, but now I had to set standards for our new relationship. I still loved them, but I did not have to allow them to treat me badly. I promised myself I would never lose my voice, and would hold others, as well as myself, to my relationship standards. These standards include: mutual love, loyalty, friendship, care, respect, honesty, and understanding. From now on, I was going to be in the arena with those who desired the same.

7. Clean out your relationship closet, and surround yourself with positive people.

Everyone was not willing to come up to my relationship standards. The more I grew, the more adjustments I made within my close circle. This was very difficult because I lost connections with people I felt were very close to my heart. However, I unwillingly let them exit because they were emotionally toxic, and I could no longer entertained the negative energy surrounding them.

Sometimes people just aren't willing to do the work—and you have to love them from a distance. As I continued to transform, the people who remained in my close circle were transforming with me, and our relationship grew stronger. I knew God would keep those who needed to be there. What surprised me the most was the new relationships I began to form with many beautiful people who walked in the same purpose. When I began to believe I deserved better, I received better. Some people accused me of being self-centered, stuck-up, etc. However, these people were not ready to accept my truth, because who I am today, contradicts who I was in my past. For this reason, I began to pick and choose who I shared this journey with, because not everyone appreciated the newfound me.

8. Be mindful of the familiar behaviors that keeps you connect with broken people.

In many of my previous relationships, I found myself trying to patch up other people's broken heart, only to have my heart used as a sacrifice. I was no longer willing to offer myself to anyone, because *my focus was on healing myself.* I couldn't keep giving away broken pieces of myself. If I felt the needed to help them, I was careful not to use myself as a sacrifice, nor feel obligated to do it. It is important I am aware of the emotional baggage that can suck me into an emotional shipwreck. Some people are comfortable in their pain, and may do whatever it takes to keep you stuck with them. They are so focused on their own dysfunctional cycle they become heavy loads. If you are not careful, they will keep you connected to whatever you are trying to free yourself from. The most difficult task was accepting I can't fix people unless they want to fix themselves. I had to give myself permission to leave it to them.

9. Write a promise letter to yourself and to God.

I wrote a promise letter to myself as I continued to discover my dreams, goals, strengths, and beauty. Because I was now able to visualize all of my dreams and desires, I was ready to pursue them. I was at a place in my life where I no longer fake my happiness, because it constantly overflows. Nothing I have experienced has the power to take it away. Although I am still dealing with the repercussion of the financial abuse, I know God has my back.

Wow! I have to say, glory to God, because to him I owe all praise. I continue to post my letter on my mirror, and carry a copy with me so I can review it whenever I feel discouraged. I would often update it when I had accomplishments and/or new goals. I still write letters to God, and I tell him about my goals, and what I am willing to do, as well as what I need him to do for me. It was my faith that restored me, and I knew everything I wanted to do was already done, and I to live as if everything had already manifested.

As I come to the end of this journey I can say without hesitation, I have fully transformed. When my daddy left me, he took my crown with him. However, as a woman who has been mended, I have been able to go back and find where he buried it. I shed layers of guilt, shame, and pain. I physically felt my transformation. Before I knew it, I felt so light, like I was lifted up and running on air. Right then, I knew God's presence was strong, and I felt myself wrapped in his arms. Every day I wear my crown, I know that I am worthy of it. Back when I wasn't quite ready to wear my crown, I wore it anyway. Yes, I had some days where I needed to reboot and relearn the meaning of my worth. However, I found myself stuck for only a day, where before I had been *stuck for a lifetime*.

It is my hope as you follow my journey you have also been doing some work on your own. As I stood with my crown, embracing my freedom, I knew this was the end of one journey, but the beginning of another.

Now that I have accepted what God has called me to do, I prepare for it, because it is not about me as much as it was about you. Are you ready to crown yourself Queen? Nothing is more refreshing than witnessing a broken woman be restored as she comes into loving herself. I have helped these women on a very small scale, but I can't wait to witness groups of women heal as they discover their crowns. I am eager to share with woman across the world how I became free, because so many women may not have the courage to do the work on their own.

Soon I hope to be standing before groups of women sharing the message that God has given me. I believe when the timing is right, God will allow this to fall into place. Today as I wait, I am blessed because I have become a Queen. This is such an empowering moment, because I am no longer just a fatherless daughter, I am a woman who has evolved.

CHAPTER 12:

A Queen in Waiting

I accept I am a woman who desires marriage, but it doesn't mean I will subject myself to anything that is not good. I am a Christian woman who desires a Christian husband who is willing to love me the way I am worthy. I refuse to settle for anything less than what I was designed to be. I give myself freedom to love God first, myself second, and everything falling in order after that. From this day forward, no man would ever come before God, me, or my happiness. I will not love in desperation, because I am now a Queen in waiting.

A Queen in Waiting

I was finally transformed from a wounded child into a vibrant, victorious Queen. When people first noticed this transformation, they said I am glowing, and want to know who the new love interest was. Everytime, I got many interesting facial expressions when I said her name is Sonja. People were mistaking my newfound love for myself for one of a new love interest. Some thought I was crazy because they can't understand why I was so happy with *being in love with one's self*. I even heard words like self-absorbed, stuck-up, selfish, and self-centered. If you have recently found your crown and established your self-worth, I'm sure you can relate to my experience. Nevertheless, I am thankful for getting to this place.

When I found myself at the end of my healing journey, I was ready to enter a stage of waiting. As a Queen in waiting, I felt worthy of love, and I am at peace because I do not have to settle for a man who is not worthy of my heart. I feel no urgency, and I am not afraid to be alone because I actually allowed myself to heal. I am no longer seeking love in a state of desperation, nor am I concerned about searching for a King. Today the crown I wear sends out a strong message saying I have standards. I am very mindful of who I entertain, because I refuse to revert to accepting men who are not willing to honor my crown.

When a man approaches me, I can now tell within a few minutes if he is willing to meet my standards. If he is not up to my standards, I have no problem releasing him. Unworthy men still approached me, and a few did try to put me to the test. There was one who really tired hard to deceive my as he preyed on the Sonja who had not yet been fully healed. He even tried to force me into a relationship but God intervened opened my eyes. I stood my ground and embraced my crown and he realized the Queen in me, and moved on. Satan tried to trick me in the middle of my healing process, but I passed the test. I am still single by choice, but I am ready for a healthy relationship because I am secure, confident, and love myself enough to wait patiently. Although a companion would be nice, I feel no urgency. If you, too, are a Queen in waiting, stop and take a moment to praise God for your victory, because this is something to be celebrated. I hope you realize the best is yet to come. So sit back, relax, and read about the *dos and don'ts* of a Queen in waiting. Use this as a reference, because one day you will be ready to receive your King.

The Dos and Don'ts of a Queen in waiting:

1. Do: Focus on living and enjoying life.

Slow down and embrace the special moments in your life, like reading a book to your child, being peaceful, enjoying a walk in the park, etc. You have only one chance to live your life. Now it is time for you to live it how you want to. Let your happiness flow from within, and find out what brings you peace and joy. Don't be afraid to spend some time alone. Some of my best moments in life were when I was alone, doing something to brought me joy. Besides, you are never really alone, because God is with you. I would rather be a happy single woman than as broken woman stuck in unhappiness. Find time to laugh every day. You can focus on so many things while you are busy living. So go and find some beautiful flowers to smell.

2. Don't: Let people pressure you into the dating scene.

Take advantage of life's precious moments, because you are no longer in a rush. Release any anxiety, and allow God to be in control. Begin dating when you are ready to date. People mean well; however, don't do anything for the pleasure of anyone else. If you want to wait, wait. Don't be afraid to tell people you want to save yourself for someone you feel is worthy of who you are. Most people will respect your wishes, and allow you the freedom wait. However, some other people want to see you with someone, or think they have the perfect guy for you. Thank them, and remain firm on your decision.

3. Don't: Be afraid to admit you are in a period of healing.

If you are just beginning the healing process, don't fool yourself into thinking you were suddenly healed by a magic wand. Relax and let the healing flow. You have spent years emotionally wounded.

Sometimes you will be tested, pressured, and almost forced to revert to loving in a broken heart. Rely on your support system, and take care of you. Our emotional health needs maintaining like a car needs an oil change. If you find yourself back in the same situation, don't panic, walk your way back out. Remember what you already lost, what you have gained, and what you have stored up for your future.

4. Do: create a list of standards before you begin dating.

You will need to set the standards, and know the worthiness of your heart. What standards do you require, for example, do you want him to be educated, have a job, be a man of God, love children, take care of his health, etc.? Determine your standards and write them down. No one is perfect, so your standards must be reasonable. However, don't make too many adjustments, and settle for someone who won't appreciate your growth, accomplishments, or self-esteem. They will never appreciate you, and the relationship will only end in your heart being further broken. Besides, when you settle for a broken man who has no respect for you or your accomplishments, they often feel intimidated and may look for ways to knock you off your feet. I spent a lot of time trying to prove to abusive men I did not think I was better than them. I would often dummy myself down, and I let them strip me of my accomplishments so they could feel good about themselves. If a man truly loves you, he will respect your standards, as long as they are reasonable.

5. Do: Define your purpose for dating.

Be honest with yourself and state your purpose for dating upfront. Decide what you want in a relationship. If you desire a marriage and children, don't waste your time dating a man who vows to never marry, because he is not worthy of your love. If you have this established upfront, it would be easier to walk away when he is not interested in giving you what you desire. If you are over twenty-five, and looking to get married, I believe every man you date should know whether or not he has a desire to be married. Don't be afraid to ask this man what intent his has in a dating relationship.

It should be one of the first conversations on your first date. I am not ashamed to say I desire love and companionship. However, I had to be honest with myself and admit I desired to be someone's wife. I want to be the apple of my husband's eye. I knew I had to realize I was worthy, and omit the foolishness getting in the way of honoring my desire. God designed me to be a wife, not a girlfriend, so I refuse to settle for anything less than what I was designed to be.

6. Do: make sure you have stopped loving in emotional dysfunction.

Make sure you are engaging in healthy relationships with friends and family before you start dating. If you truly desire to be in love, make sure you are ready for it when it comes. Pay attention to how you interact and resolve conflicts. Set relationship standards with those who are in your close circle and stick to them. Make a commitment to yourself that you will not take part in any relationship not meeting your standards. This will help you stay balanced if you find you are still struggling with your self-worth. If you are having trouble finding your voice in your close circle, it *may not be time* for you to date. It doesn't mean it's going to take years, it means you've still got a little more self-work to do. You don't want to spend anymore of your life waiting on the wrong man to finally love you back. So before you try to love again, make sure you are whole. Don't sugarcoat the drama. Get in the habit dealing with it.

7. Do: Take yourself out on dates.

Find out what you like to do, take yourself out on a date, and do it. Ask a sister or good friend to do a girlfriend's night out once a month so you can become familiar with being in a fancy restaurant, a social environment, or a community activity. Keep yourself aware of what going on so you maintain an interest in things outside of your children and your household. Find out what and where you like to eat. Write down a list of restaurants and one to visit once a month. Treat yourself like you want a man to treat you so you become comfortable with being treated well. Find out what things

A Queen in Waiting

you can do by yourself, for example, go to a play, opera, show, etc..

8. Do: study the act of love while you are in waiting.

Learn about love while you are a Queen in waiting. Be observant and study how people love around you. Ask questions of other women in successful relationships, and listen to how they did it. Watch how men and women interact. Sit in a park or another romantic place, and study relationships. Pay attention to how men treat women, and ask yourself if this is what you would like in your relationship. Look for red flag clues as men approach you, even though your intent is not to date at this time. Surround yourself with emotionally healthy people, and observe how they love.

9. Don't: accept anything less than a King

Accept you have become with woman of standards, and you do not have to accept a relationship because it falls in your lap. If you see the red flags, acknowledge them, and don't feel obligated to go out with a man simply because he asked. When someone asks you out, tell him you will think about it so you can truly have time to think about it. If he does not meet your any of standards, thank him and keep moving. When you believe you deserve a King, others will too. In the past, I was talked into a relationship before I could realize the red flags. Today I won't go out with anyone unless they have potential and meet some of standards. I know after the first date if I am willing to continue. If he disregards marriage, religion, or children, I know I need not invest any more time in dating him. I pay attention to the emotional baggage they carry, and I read the red flags long before he presents himself to me.

10. Do: make sure you review the dating checklist when you are ready to date.

Here are some general dating tools to assist you when you feel you are ready to date. This could be the difference between finding a King—and ending up with another abuser.

The Queen's Dating Checklist

- Pay attention to his morals, values, and religious beliefs. If he does not share that same beliefs and morals as you, this will definitely be an issue that will present itself later on.

- Pay attention to his appearance. How well does he take care of himself? Check his fingernails, hair, body odor, teeth, etc. I know this sounds crazy, but his appearance can be an indication of homelessness, substance abuse, mental illness, etc.

- Listen with all of your senses. Sometimes we let our heart blindly guide us. Listen to his views on life. How does he feel about marriage, women's roles, children, etc.? If his views seem distorted, chances are they are. When he says something alarming, don't ignore it. He is letting you know who he is.

- Check his personal history. If he passes step one, you need to find out more about him. Find out about his criminal history, if he lived in other states, if he was married before, etc. You can find some of this by asking him directly. If he is honest, he will tell you everything you need to know. If he seems secretive, proceed with caution and consider this a red flag. If he has a criminal history, it may be wise to end your pursuit.

- Ask about his family history. If you are thinking about getting serious, you need to see how he interacts with his family. Pay ttention to how they treat each other. If you spend enough time paying attention in the beginning, you will be able to pick up on unusual behaviors. If a man still lives with his mother, and he is in his mid-twenties, something is wrong.

- Find out about his work history and employment record. A man who has had multiple jobs in a short time span may have some stability issues. This could also indicate he is short tempered, has commitment issues, or has a difficult time socializing with people, or has trouble staying employed.

- Ask about his previous commitments, such as if he has ever been married, been in a long-term relationship, or has children. This could be another great conversation piece during the

A Queen in Waiting

early stages of dating. A man over 40, who has never been married or in a serious relationship, could have commitment issues. A man who has a healthy relationship with his children is more likely to be a potential mate than a man who does not acknowledge his role as a father.

- Pay attention to those in his social group. Are they in committed relationships? If his best friend introduces you to different women within a short time period, this may indicate his friend is a womanizer. Don't be afraid to bring this up in a private conversation to get a feel of his view about where he wants your relationship to go. Remember, birds of a feather flock together.

- Be aware of his motives in the beginning. If he is trying to rush you into a commitment only after a few dates, run. This strongly indicates he is someone who likes is be in control. A person, who likes to be in control, will want to maintain control very early at any cost, even abuse.

- Stay away from men who have excessive baggage. If he has not been able to resolve the issues from his previous relationship, chances are they will become issues with you. The best thing you can do in this situation is to offer a distant friendship. You can't allow yourself to be with someone *you need to fix*.

- If any of his characteristics remind you of domestic abuse (see Chapter 7), do not allow yourself to fall victim. Stop seeing immediately him before he becomes attached. If you find he is stalking, threatening, or harassing you, get help.

If you have read though section three, "The Mending the Pieces" and your heart still needs mending, you may need to go back and revisit each chapter. Someone or something may be keeping stuck. Let them know you have some emotional repairing to do, and when you are done, it will make you a better person. If this person has real love for you, he will understand, and may even offer to go along on your healing journey. If he doesn't he is refusing to allow you the self-work you need. Perhaps, it is because this person is afraid you will realize he has victimized you. He may believe if you love yourself too much, you may realize he is only in the relationship for his own benefit.

Making life changes is easier said than done. However, if someone is keeping you emotionally broken, only you can decide if you are going to live in it. Remember, you have the power to recreate your story. You may need to create a temporary exit so you can do some self-discovery. I am the biggest supporter of marriage. However, in cases where there is dysfunction and abuse taking a break and doing the work can be the best thing for both of you. I am not telling anyone to walk out of a marriage; however, you don't have to be broken in a relationship with someone who professes to love you. I recommend anyone in a situation where you are feeling emotionally broken, seek couples therapy, speak to your pastor, or someone who is nonbiased, and has knowledge of relationships.

Thank you for walking with me through all of the healing phases in this book. Like me, I'm sure you shared both moments of tears and moments of joy. Remember, healing is a process, and you spent many years chasing after the love and validation of your father. Although you are now a Queen in waiting, you may occasionally find yourself stuck in old patterns. I pray God continues to restore you as you find relief in knowing God is always there, and you are worthy of being loved.

Healing will always be a work in progress, but I know God is truly working on me and through me. When I think about where I am now, I am truly grateful for all God has done for me. Many days I say, "My God, how did I ever make it through everything?" I am no different from any other woman who came from the same place. I grew up poor, in the projects, and fatherless. Yes, I am ready to admit my life was far from perfect, and at times, I felt powerless. However, now that I have healed enough, it is time for me to embark on another journey. As God continues to show me my purpose, I will continue to walk in truth, and make a commitment to become an advocate helping to heal the effects of fatherless.

In the final section of this book, the focus now shifts to helping the younger generation repair their pain. I don't know exactly how I will do this, but as long as I am willing, God will guide me.

HE WHO FIRST HELD HER HEART

PART IV:

Hearts Unbroken

Chapter 13:
What's a Daddy to Do, and Mommy, Too!

Chapter 14:
What About the Fallen Princess?

Chapter 15:
Letters to Their Daughters

Chapter 16:
Who Will Fill Those Empty Shoes?

This section, "Hearts Unbroken," focuses on changing the fatherless epidemic, and helping fathers build stronger relationships with their daughters. It also addresses the fatherless community, encouraging both men and women to become sensitive to the needs of our fatherless generation. It includes many beautiful love letters written by fathers to their daughters, and the book ends with my own search for change and healing the children who continue to be impacted by fatherless.

CHAPTER 13:

What's a Daddy to Do, and Mommy, Too?

Dedicated to daddies and daughters

Daddy, I need you…

Daddy, I need you to love me and show me you care.

I need you to tuck me in at night or maybe brush my hair.

I need you to protect me and make me feel secure.

I need to know when I'm afraid my daddy will be there.

I need you to teach about the beauty I have inside.

When Mommy shows me how to be a woman, I need you to teach me pride.

"Why does my daughter keep running away, acting out, dressing like a slut, and trying to date when she is only thirteen?" he asked, as his daughter sat next to him with her arms crossed and eyes rolling at every word. "I have given her everything—clothes, shoes, nice schools—but she doesn't appreciate any of it." Before he could finish, her frustration escaped, and she blurted out, "But did I ask for any of it?" He glared at her, looking disappointed, as she continued. "All you do is yell at me, and tell me I can't do nothing right. You used to say you love me when I was little, but you don't now. All you care about is your life and work, but I'm just there. I hate being there."

How can a daddy make sure he validates his little princess so she is able to grow into a woman who is emotionally secure and intact? You have heard this often enough, but "teen girls who feel abandoned by their fathers will seek out other ways of interacting with the opposite sex in an effort to fulfill their developmental need to be loved and validated." What's a daddy to do? Every daughter needs to know she is protected, loved, and supported by her father. Sometimes fathers assume their mere presence in the home is enough. By now you realize love has little to do with the financial support many fathers provide. It has more to do with the emotional and physical presence.

Unfortunately, I see many families in my private practice where the father has misunderstood his role, and has allowed himself to become only "the provider." It is not until his daughter begins to act out does he realize what she has been missing. In many of the cases, she is well aware she is longing for her daddy's love. Before you allow your baby girl to grow up and fall in love with any other man, you should be the first man to *hold her heart*. How you nurture her heart will determine what she thinks of herself, her self-image, and her self-worth. As a mother teaches her how to be a lady, it is her father who shows her how a lady should be treated. It is through her daddy's eyes she gains an understanding of her place in the world, how the world will receive her, and how she is to be loved by her mate.

A daddy can do many simple things to assure that his daughter knows she is loved and validated. He teaches her how valuable she is to him by spending quality time with her, by listening to her, and by making her feel protected by him. He captures special moments with her, and pays attention to her interests so she knows she has gained the stamp of approval from daddy. He makes sure at the end of the day, his princess feels like the most beautiful, special girl in the world. Not only does she need to be validated by you, she needs to see you validate her mother, or your significant other. How you also treat your wife teaches your daughter how men should treat her. You can't tell your baby girl she's important, and later she witnesses you disrespect her mother. It is impossible to be a good daddy and be a womanizer at the same time.

As she grows up and faces adolescence, she may migrate through periods of self-doubt, self-esteem, and even dislike of her physical appearance. When her daddy reinforces her beauty, she will appreciate it even if she can't tell him right then. If you are a father, and have been meaning to spend more time with your daughter, stop putting it off, and start now. If you are not sure about your relationship with your daughter, take a moment and do a quick assessment of your daddy-daughter relationship.

- How have you captured her heart?
- Did you tuck her in a night, and tell her she is loved?
- Did you make her feel protected her when she is afraid?
- Does she know you are listening to her?
- Does she know how much she means to you?

Whenever I hear the song by Beyoncé about her daddy, I sometimes get a little emotional. "I want my first-born son to be like my daddy." Those are some very powerful words. I listened to the whole song so many times, and based on this song, it was obvious this woman was in love with her daddy. I don't mean love in a weird, inappropriate way. Do you know the relationship you have with your daughter determines who she becomes as an adult? It also determines if she is be likely to be involved with drugs, suicide, sexual abuse, sexual exploitation, criminal activity, and domestic violence? Your presence and emotional involvement will help your daughter have a healthy self-esteem, avoid risky behaviors, and be less likely to be victimized.

Here are some suggestions to help build a stronger bond with your daughter. While she is very young, the simple things requiring little effort can entertain her for hours. Spending time with her daddy during those simple moments and small milestones will impact her for a lifetime. Listed below are activities you can do with your daughter who is between preschool and preteen. As she gets older, her interests will change. However, some daughters may continue to enjoy these activities, even as teenagers.

Father Daughter Activities:
- Pick a favorite father-daughter song.
- Do an art project together.
- Go on a bike ride.
- Play a board game.
- Cook a meal for Mom.
- Take her to a male sporting, event like golfing, fishing, etc.
- Take her to a father-daughter dance.
- Walk or drive her to school.
- Take her to work with you.
- Take a "sick day" together, and do something fun.
- Let her paint your fingernails or toenails.
- Take her shopping for something special.
- Let her pick an activity she considers fun.
- Comb her hair and learn to put it in a ponytail or braid it.
- Attend at least one Girl Scout meeting with her.
- Chaperone a field trip.
- Give her a hug, and a kiss her at least three time a day.
- Take her to a professional sports event.

- Help her with her homework or special project.
- Ask her about her day.
- Go on a daddy-daughter road trip together.
- Read to her, or let her see you read.
- Go to the library or museum together.
- Play dress-up with her.
- Bake a cake together.
- Watch a movie with her.
- Go for a walk, hike, or run.
- Discipline her and make sure you are fair and firm.
- Let her know you are there for her.
- Listen to her concerns.

One day Daddy's little princess will grow up to be her own Queen. As she matures, she needs to learn what it means to be Queen. It is very important a teenage girl learns how to interact in healthy relationships with the opposite sex, other than her daddy. The more independent she becomes, you have to find other ways of bonding with her. This is the time to allow her to have a choice in the activities and a way of learning her interest and hobbies.

Here are some ways a father can bond with his teenage daughter:

- Be there with her as she transitions from a little girl into a young lady; it is important you teach her about her beauty, and about her voice. She will look to you for validation as she searches for her definition of herself. If you remind her she is beautiful inside and out, she will believe it because her daddy told her it was so.
- Encourage her to develop her talents. If she is a singer, encourage her to participate in the church choir or school performance and attend them.
- If she is into sports, you have to be her biggest cheerleader. Practice her game with her, and help her perfect her skills.
- Let her know the importance of her education, and expose her to various universities and colleges. Plan a college road trip for

the two of you and throw in some fun activities like a shopping day, etc.
- Encourage her to start thinking about her lifelong dream and educational pursuit and guide her on her road to success.
- Stay connected with her social circle, and learn who her friends are.
- Pay attention to how she views herself in the world, and what events triggers certain emotions like laughter, sadness, anger, etc.
- Don't let anyone teach her about boys except you. Although this conversation may be tough, tell her the truth about friendships, relationships, and sex. Allow her to express her interest in the opposite sex. Use this as an opportunity to teach her how to read the red flags, and how to know when she has really found a good guy.
- Take her on daddy-daughter dates, and show her how to demand respect while on a date. Show her the basics of etiquette, and how men are supposed to treat women, and let her know she doesn't have to accept anything less than the best treatment.
- Help her develop a strong sense of self by reminding her how proud you are of her, and how much you love her.
- Show her how to be strong mentally, spiritually, and emotionally.
- Allow her to have a voice and to express when she is angry, sad, or happy.
- Teach her how to protect herself physically, and show her how to defend herself if she is approached with danger.
- Send her special unannounced gifts like candy, stuffed animals, or flowers to remind her how much she means to you. It doesn't have to be any special day.
- Write her a love letter expressing your feelings, or get her a promise gift on a special birthday, for example, a promise ring on her thirteenth birthday to acknowledge her transition. This is something she will cherish for a lifetime.

Dads, I know it can be tough letting your little princess transition into a woman. However, it you interfere with her transition, it can be detrimental to your relationship, and she may run into the arms of someone who you worked so hard for her to avoid. It is important you allow her to find herself as she evolves, and trust you have given her the tools to make the right decisions. Be open, and try to understand her view as she chooses things that may not be your choice for her. Watch closely, but allow the maturity to produce the confident, strong, and secure young woman you have created.

A note to single mother's

If you are a single mother, realize you can't do this on your own. Be willing to reach out for support through your family, church, community, and/or the school. Research what's available within your area. No one is expecting you to play the role of her father, because it is impossible. You can be the best mother in the world, but you still cannot fill the shoes of a father. If at all possible, try to have a workable parenting relationship with her father so she has the benefit of both of you. Do this only if he is able to engage in a nonthreatening, healthy relationship with her. Give him the opportunity to father her, and make sure you are not pushing him out of her life because of unresolved issues with your own father and/or him.

It is a fact that fatherless daughters become single mothers, who have fatherless daughters who become single mothers.

If this is the case, please try to resolve your own abandonment issues. Be willing to break the cycle by healing yourself and giving you daughter the opportunity to have her father or a father figure in her life. It is important you seek professional counseling and/or spiritual guidance to help guide you. If you interfere with the relationship between your daughter and her father, you are contributing to a lifelong feeling of abandonment and the resulting ramifications. You have to be able to rise above your own pain, and realize *it is no longer about you*. It's about your children needing their daddy. It does not matter if he is now living with the woman with whom he cheated on you. He may have not been the best mate, but has the potential as a good father.

I speak on this because as a single mom, I realized there was a time when I was using my pain from my relationship with my children's father as a barrier to keep him from them. Because he had hurt me, I convinced myself he would also hurt my children. I had to allow him the room to establish himself as a father. Although he had difficulties on his part, I knew I had done my best to support their relationship. If it is not possible for her father to be involved, make sure you allow your daughter an opportunity to engage in healthy relationships with a male role model who you know and trust.

Because her father is absent, she will learn from you by following in your footsteps.

Here is a list of guidelines for single moms:

- Respect her and respect yourself by setting an example.
- Don't let your daughter see you treated badly by anyone, not even her father.
- Always wear your crown around her, and show her how it is supposed to be worn.
- Don't allow anyone to threaten your self-worth.
- Be open and talk to her about healthy relations and share your mistakes.
- Tell her about predators and those who seek to bring harm to her and teach her how to recognize the red flags, and read the signs of abuse.
- Get to know her friends and her social group, and stay connected and meet their parents.
- You can also do mother-daughter activities as well.

The more you engage with you daughter, the more likely she is to desire healthy relationships and avoid risk-taking activities. Staying involved is the key.

Below is a recap of some of the dos and don'ts:

1. Do seek family counseling for the two of you so both can have a place to express your feelings surrounding her absent father.

2. Do stay involved with family, church, and the community so your daughter has the opportunity to interact with other girls and their fathers.

3. Do ask for help from uncles, cousins, granddads, pastors, coaches, teachers, etc. Seek help from anyone who has demonstrated he can be a positive and trustworthy male role model.

4. Do keep her involved with activities at school, church, and in the community so she has little alone and unsupervised free time.

5. If you are dating, make sure you check this man's background and know who he is before you consider bringing them around her. You do not want to subject her to domestic violence or any kind of abuse, including sexual abuse.

6. Don't get involved with a man who refuses to accept her. You are a package deal, and she must know she matters more than your relationship with him.

7. Don't bring a potential daddy around until you are sure he is willing to be there, and take on the full responsibly of husband and father.

8. Don't involve yourself in relationships where men treat you poorly. Maintain healthy relationships.

A note to absent fathers

When a man is not able to fill the "father" shoes, he leaves behind children who feel abandoned and brokenhearted. Perhaps, you yourself experienced some form of fatherlessness. It's no secret that the fatherlessness epidemic has gone from one generation to the next. However, society expects fatherless children to grow up and become productive parents—without knowing half of their identity. Fatherlessness not only has a devastating impact on your daughters, it also has a devastating impact on your sons because they sometimes become the next generation of absent fathers. They too become immune to the significant role of a father, and they will produce children without considering the lives of *those* children or their role as a father.

If you are an absent father, I hope you have begun to understand the importance of your role in your child's life. If you have sons and daughters you have lost touch with, please reach out to your community, church, etc., so you can get help integrating back into the lives of you children. If you don't have a good connection with their mother, it doesn't mean you have to forgo the relationship with your children. Don't assume your children are getting along well without you. This is absolutely *not true*.

If you are looking to mend the relationship with your daughter or son, many programs exist to help fathers learn how to be actively involved. If your relationship with your daughter needs repairing, know it is never too late to start the process. The healing is necessary, and can take place at any moment. It doesn't matter if she's two or thirty years old, she still desires to be loved by her daddy. Asking for forgiveness can be difficult. Sometimes it appears the easiest resolution is to sweep the past under the rug and pretend it never happened. I am not saying asking for forgiveness guarantees you will instantly receive it. However, I will say you owe it to her at the least, acknowledge the abandonment. If you are strong enough to admit these things to her, you have made a major step in helping your daughter mend her wounds. This could be the beginning of the restoration of your father-daughter relationship. I know it takes courage. However, you can start by initiating a simple conversation with her. Once you have started the process of communication, you are well on your way to healing for both of you.

Some of these helpful steps may lead to repairing the damage. It is important you acknowledge the hurt you caused in her heart, and recognize you must also do some repair.

Here is a list of things you can do to repair your relationship:

1. Ask her what you can do to repair the damage. Try to get an understanding of what she needs from you right now.

2. Give her time to think about it. She may not know how to respond right away.

3. Be willing to listen to what she has to say about the pain you have caused, and affirm her pain, and validate her feelings.

4. Allow her to determine if she wants to engage in a relationship with you. She may not be ready to forgive right away.

5. Don't give up on her. Keep trying to reach her, and try to understand she is coming from a broken place.

6. Make sure you are there to stay. The last thing she needs is to have you cause further injury to her.

7. Don't expect to jump in as a disciplinarian after you have been absent for several years. Before you can discipline her, you must first develop a relationship with her.

8. Be patient, and don't give up.

9. Go to family counseling, or get support from friends and family.

10. Love her anyway.

CHAPTER 14:

What About the Fallen Princess?

Fallen Princess

Society doesn't understand your pain or your desire to be seen.

You paint your face, believing it will lead you to what you think love means.

You think you've found someone to replace the love missing from you dad.

He buys you pretty dresses and gives you all the things you never had.

Happiness doesn't last too long because this love soon cuts so deep.

Now you hid in dark alleys, and walk up and down the busy streets.

Deep inside, you hide your battered heart, which has grown far too old.

It carried the burden of all the pain from the many stories you never told.

Your eyes have seen it all, and your body has been so misused.

The pain forces you to grow up too fast, leaving your young mind confused.

What About the Fallen Princess?

"Breaking news: Child sex trafficking has been on a steady increase right here Milwaukee, Wisconsin," said a voice as it pierced my eardrums. I was listening to Fox 6 news while preparing for work. Suddenly I turned to the TV and saw abandoned houses, dark alleys, flashing police lights, and men in handcuffs. What intrigued me the most were the blurred-out images of the young girls who were rescued. I couldn't see their faces, but I was familiar with their pain because it somehow resonated with me. These were girls as young as twelve years old who had been dragged into this newfound definition of slavery. Many of them were runaways who had been snatched from the streets, and then sold for sex. Some had been missing for several years, even traveling between states. Working in the largest urban school district in the state has allowed me to see some of this first-hand. However, I was unaware of the statistics until I begin to research the fatherless epidemic.

I began to discover more than I expected, and was taken aback because this was the first time I was able to connect the dots. A lot of girls and woman I interviewed admitting to being involved in prostitution, stripping, and child pornography in their past. Most intriguing was the fact *all of them were fatherless*. It doesn't mean all fatherless daughters will become victims of a sex trafficking ring, etc. it simply proves that girls who are victims of the sex trafficking ring are more than likely to be girls searching for the love of their fathers. Their longing and desperation lead down the road of self-exploitation.

I did not do any official research, but most of my information comes from the survey and interviews I conducted in my private practice. Before I began writing this book, I was disconnected and completely unaware of the effects of fatherlessness. Although I worked with young girls and women involved in prostitution, domestic violence, and sexual abuse, etc., it wasn't until I was forced to face my own fatherlessness that *I had an epiphany* and began to notice the obvious connections. The more I came into my own awareness, the more I began to be awakened by the tragedies surrounding me. I couldn't help but think about all of the young girls who had crossed my path who had been misjudged, mistreated, and overlooked by people, even myself.

I have worked in the public school system for fourteen years, and as educators, we are exposed to the realities of the world. Yes, I stood along with others who judged the mother who came into the school looking like she had come from walking the street. I made a call or two to Child Protective Services about the twelve-year-old girl who was pregnant by an adult man, and the fourteen-year-old who bragged about her pimp. Although I was helping them, secretly I had judged them. I was blinded by my own self-righteousness, until I faced myself. I quickly realized I was no different from any of them because, like me, they, too, were desperately searching for the love of their father. Once I was honest about my fatherlessness, I connected with them, and I was able to reach out to many of them. When the girl knew I shared the same pain driving her, she trusted me and shared her experience. Over the past few years, I have been reaching out more because I truly desire to help them. I no longer judge them for their circumstances. Today I embrace them, cry with them, hug them, and love them.

How do we help her?

What do you say to her when you see her wearing inappropriate clothing, unaware that she exposing herself? Do you scold her and shame her, or do you embrace her, love her, and teach her self-worth? Many of you have seen young girls within your reach who are struggling with their sense of self—and we respond by doing nothing. How many times have you turned your head and allowed her to face the world without the love and validation she needs to love herself? Because her view of womanhood is distorted, she is vulnerable, and is more likely to be captured by the deceptions of sexual exploiter.

In exchange for her crown, she mimics the degrading roles of prostitute, stripper, exotic dancer, escort, etc. She becomes a young girl living in the fast lane. As a result of her experiences, she appears vicious, but if you handle her gently, she is as delicate as a wilted flower. On the inside of her hardened shell is a wounded heart broken in many pieces. If we ignore her, she will eventually stumble into the hand of someone who acknowledges her brokenness by making false promises to love her. He is capable of capturing her before we realize she has slipped through our fingers.

Where do we begin to help her? If we do nothing, this lifestyle will continue to worsen as she becomes a part of the repetitive cycle, and models it for the generation following behind her.

- We can begin by acknowledging the generations of abandoned daughters and changing society's negative view of them.
- We have to reach out to her and help her to discover her worth as we educate her.
- We can teach young boys around her to appreciate and respect what it means to be a woman, and teach them how to be men.

As a female role model

If you are a woman who is looking to help, I am sure a young girl is within your reach desperately in search of love. Take her under your wing and embrace her while you become her example. Show her how a woman can express her beauty and be respected.

Perhaps you can donate several hours a month to spend one-on-one time with her talking about boys, fashion, relationships, etc. You can share your experiences, and let her know she doesn't have to choose the path she's now on. Encourage her to reach for her dreams, get an education, and maybe even attend college. Let her know what life is like as a successful, strong, confident woman. Help her to find a positive male role model in her life so she can help learn how to have healthy relationships with the opposite sex. If she already has an involved parent, include them, ask them what they think she needs, and try to help them find additional support.

Filling the father's role

If you are a man trying to fill the role of a father, beware of the inappropriate reactions you may get from her. Because of her past, her misinterpretation of your love for her could cause her to respond to you in a sexual way. Remember, you are the one in a position of power, and should redirect her by letting her know you are not seeking any sexual gratification from her. If she does not understand your role is simply to be a mentor, you may want to interact with her when other adults are involved—or not at all. It can be as simple as inviting her to participate in some of the daddy-daughter activities you do with your own daughter. If you don't have any daughters, team up with a buddy or brother who has a daughter until you have established a relationship with her and her mother.

Make sure you stay connected to her family, and never spend time with her without first getting their approval. Some girls may withdraw and become wary of men because of their fear of being hurt or abandoned. She may even lash out, become angry, or push you away because she does not trust your intent. As she becomes familiar with you, continue to engage with her on her terms so she can learn to trust you. She will be guarded and more than likely will reject your invitations. This may be her way of protecting herself from what is unfamiliar. I recommend you reach out only to young girls you have already established a familiar relationship with, for example a niece, cousin, potential stepdaughter, goddaughter, etc.

Here are a list tips for men who want to fill the father's role for fatherless daughters:

1. Make sure you clearly define your intentions. Some may mistake your fatherly role as an attempt to sexually exploit young girls.

2. Be careful, and set clear boundaries before you engage, and don't ever cross those boundaries. Be careful not to engage in any inappropriate conversations, not even jokingly.

3. Be aware of the sensitive nature of your relationship. Assume she may have been sexually abused and/or have witnessed mistreatment of women. Be mindful of her fragile heart.

4. Do not commit to being a surrogate father unless you have the time to invest in it. The last thing she needs is to be abandoned by another daddy.

5. Make sure you involve her mother and your significant other so everyone is aware and understands your intentions with this young girl.

These tips are not intended for misuse or an opportunity for a predator to gain the trust of a young victim and/or her family. I suggest mothers do a criminal background check, talk to people in the community, and further investigate any adult who wants to engage with their daughter.

A note to stepfathers

If you are a stepdad, please do not exclude yourself from the daddy role. Your role is very important, even if she does have a relationship with her father. Don't sit on the sidelines—you can help her parents raise her because she needs you, too. Pay attention to how you treat her mother because she will learn the most from the man who is in her home. As you know, when you married her mother, you also became married to the relationship with her children. If their biological father is absent, you owe it to your stepdaughter to be the real dad that she needs. She may not reach out to you, or may not think you can fulfill the role of her real daddy. Prove her wrong, because you can still love and validate her.

Rather, you are her stepfather, uncle, cousin, godfather, etc., your willingness to help this fallen princess will teach her how to validate herself as she transitions into womanhood. If she doesn't understand the significance of her father's absence, it doesn't mean she hasn't been affected by it. It may appear as if she has become immune to love, and doesn't know how to respond to it. However, love her anyway, because you loving her unconditionally will teach her the meaning of a father-daughter's love. If you are looking for ways to bond with her, please refer to Chapter 13, "What's a Daddy to Do, and Mommy, Too," for a list of ideas. Regardless of how old she is, she is still a little girl who needs to know she's special, beautiful, valuable, loved, and protected. When she has a father figure who teaches her what it means to be validated, she too will make positive choices for herself, and will go on to seek positive relationships.

CHAPTER 15:

Letters to Their Daughters

"When a man becomes the daddy of a little princess, she pulls out the gentleness in him. Suddenly there is a soft side no one has ever been able to tap into. I have become a better man and I wanted to be a strong and protective father to her because I never knew mine."

— Montré Moore

When I first began to write this book, I did not realize how all of the father and daughter letters would impact me. At the time, I wanted to give a voice to fatherless daughters, and also positive words that would encourage them. I thought if they read letters from the many fathers, they would be able to understand the special bond between a father and daughter. It was my intent to bring the healing that I myself, had found.

What I did not realize was the power in awareness I was spreading among fathers who have daughters of various ages. It's not to say these fathers weren't aware of the love and validation their daughters needed to feel. It was an awakening of how precious their daughters were to their hearts. Some fathers said they found themselves in tears as they wrote to their precious daughters. Other fathers said they had a new appreciation and understanding of what it meant to be a daughter's father.

I am so excited to share the love many of these fathers expressed to their daughters and the pictures capturing these priceless moments of love were absolutely breathtaking. As a young girl, I had longed to hear my father say, "I love you." If I could have heard those three words, they would have made a world of a difference.

I want to give special thanks to all of the wonderful fathers who took the time to write a letter for this special project. Thank you all for sharing your honesty, love, and devotions to your daughters. Your letters brought comfort when I needed to know what it meant to experience a father's love. God bless you, and may you continue to be the wonderful fathers you have committed to be.

------------▲------------

Dear Laya,

Hi Baby. Daddy was thinking of you as I always do, and wanted to share with you what you mean to me, and how I truly love you from the core of my being. From the very first moment I saw you, I loved you more than any other. I beheld your beauty and was forever changed, and charged to a new level as a man. What your daddy is trying to say,

Baby, is your very existence brings me a joy beyond words. I never thought I would see the age of twenty-one, let alone to be able to create such a beautiful human being.

I truly believe with all of my heart the great accomplishment of my life will be being the greatest father I can be. You see, Baby, Daddy never experienced the joy of having a father. I promised myself and God if I ever became a father I would do my all to be the best I could be. So Laya, I have devoted, pledged, and sacrificed, any and everything as it relates to you and your well-being.

The happiness being your daddy brings me often leaves me speechless. I pray God's blessing over your life each and every day for I know where my abilities fall short, and his are endless. I am so thankful for you because you being in my life has given my life such value.

I am your daddy, as long as God allows me to be with you, I will always be there for you. I will always make sure your feet are covered at night with your soft cover. I will always share my food with you, even when I don't want to. I will always kiss your bumps and bruises. I will always surround you with the tools you need to grow and develop. I will always take up for you and stand behind you, but correct you in your wrong. I will always protect you. I will always give you hugs and kisses. I will always watch what you want on TV. I will be there no matter what the situation is, from a cry to a call, I will always have my senses toned to you.

Love, Daddy Montré J. Moore

▲

Dear Angel Baby,

You are my world. When you came into my life, I stopped all of the negative activity all around me. I didn't want you to see the things not meant for you to see. I wanted you to see I love you and want to be in your life because you motivate me to go down the right path so I could show you the way to success. As a young father my patience is sometimes tested, but then your smile and dimples make all of the anger melt away. It's like you know what you are doing. I think it is funny because I did the same thing when I was a child. I see myself when I look into your eyes.

I've come to realize young girls need a father figure in their lives. It's our job as fathers to give you the love and protection you need to feel secure. People have told me I'm going to be a good father because they see how much love and affection I show for you. I'm not trying to be cocky or feel like I'm better than anyone, but we need more fathers out here like myself.

Love, Your Daddy

Anonymous: 17-year-old father of an 18-month-old daughter

Dear Daughters,

I want to first thank my heavenly Father for my wonderful parents who are now deceased. We had a family of eight girls and the boys. Mama and Papa were married for 65 years before Mama passed several years before Papa passed, and later joined her in heaven. Papa worked and paid the bills, but Mama ran the house while Papa backed her up. They taught us to love and respect each other and our elders. We all loved, honored and respected Mama and Papa. Our parents were great examples of loving parents.

On June 20, 1964, your mother and I wed. This June 20, 2014, we will be married 50 years. I love her more now than the day we wed. When we married, my Sweetie had a two-year-old little girl named Tracey. So I had to get busy learning how to become a good father. I used to babysit for my sisters, but this was different. I am now a father, not an uncle. With Tracey, I went through "Daddy Boot Camp," and after a while along comes our next daughter, Felicia. I had learned with Tracey you have to be understanding, patient and that communication is paramount; yet letting our kids know you mean business simultaneously. I know when you love your children, this love helps you to parent according to their individual needs. Eddie, our son was born next, and then Heather our youngest child. We realize as parents we are so richly blessed.

One Sunday morning, December 29, 1986, I visited your mother's church when she wasn't expecting me. That day, God did some amazing things for our family and me. He restored me for I had backslidden, He delivered me from alcohol and tobacco and He filled me with the Holy Spirit. I haven't had a drink or a cigarette since. And I really learned to walk in love and become a wiser, more loving and more gracious husband and father. Hallelujah! Praise Jesus!

We have fifteen grandchildren and five great grandchildren. We tell them they are immensely loved, and we encourage them regularly. We tell them they are abundantly blessed, and they believe it. We've prayed that God will profusely bless them and their seed, and it is what we expect. God is a blesser and He wants us to be blessers also.

I am so proud of our family. It is an honor and a privilege to parent our children, and we are so grateful to God for this opportunity.

The Bible says "To train up a child in the way he should go and when he is old he will not depart from it" (Proverbs 22:6). Children are a blessing from God and very precious in His eyes. I also thank God for the women in my life, past and present: from Mama, my wonderful wife Dorothy, mother-in-law Katie, our three daughters, sisters, aunts, granddaughters, and cousins.

Edward Colbert, Sr.

Dear Makaila,

The first day I saw your face I knew my life would never be the same. Yes, I love your brother, and I'm honored to be his father. But, your entry into the world thrust me into a new realm of responsibility. Why? You represent life.

I once heard a person say that women possess the portal to earth. The only way humans can be born is by traveling through the womb of a woman. And, although you're a baby girl, I know one day you'll be a beautiful, powerful woman, equipped with life-giving potential. This means the sons and/or daughters you birth will receive love and nurturing based upon the care you receive from your mother and from me. So, the stakes are high, but I'm ready. I'm ready to grow, so I can help you grow. I'm ready to learn how to love better, so I can love you to life, love you to excellence, and love you to wholeness.

When I look into your eyes, I'm filled with delight. My spirit lights up. I know you're only five months old, and it will be a little while before you read this letter. But, it's okay. I write with joy, knowing one day you will read this letter. Hopefully it will inspire you. Hopefully, in its contents you'll find words to nourish your soul.

Makaila, inspire me. You encourage me. Your cooing makes me smile because I know you're trying to talk to me. But, don't worry. It won't be along before you can say everything you want to say. I look forward to talking to you about the sky and the sun. I can't wait to tell you about Africa. I'm eager to tell you about God and His love because when I see you, I'm convinced He's real. And, I'm certain He loves me because He blessed me with you. So glad you're in my life!

Love, Daddy

Dear baby Carter,

This is your father. Right now you are still in your mother's womb. I dreamed about a little girl so I hope the dream was about you. However, we won't find out for sure until later today. Either way, I will love you the same. Although my dad wasn't there for me, I vow to be there for you until the end of time. I want to teach you the word of God, how to pray day and night, and how to let God guide you. I can't wait until you finally come out so I can hold you, comfort you, and never let you go. You are your daddy and mommy's blessed baby. I can't wait to hear your little feet running around the house. LOL! You are always going to be daddy's special gift from God above. I never received hugs, pats on the back, or words of encouragements when I was a child. However, the day you arrive, I will give you all I never had—my entire love! The thought of you makes me happy. We are trying to get everything together for you. Lord's willing, I want to take you to toy stores, county fairs, on vacations, to church, and a lot more. I'm back in school and working every day trying to provide and support you and your mommy.

Baby Carter, daddy wants you to know I love you so much already. I'm going to give you so many things I never had. God showed me you before you ever came, so I know you're going to be the greatest blessing we ever had.

Love your father,

To my precious daughters, Amyrel and Charity,

First of all, I want you to know I love you both and miss you dearly. I want to apologize for the circumstances that resulted in our separation. I hope you don't ever think or feel like I just left you. I always have, and always will, make the ultimate sacrifice for both of you, no matter what the consequences.

However, for this situation it would not benefit you if I'm not longer able to continually give you the love and protection you need. I want you girls to know even though I am not with you, everything I do is for you. Know I am here whenever you need me. I want you to know I love you, and always will. I would do anything to change this situation if I could.

You girls are both very special and very special to me. You are my little princesses.

Love your daddy, Tyrone

(These people were affected by Hurricane Katrina. The mother and children went to Atlanta, he to Texas. Eventually he returned to New Orleans from Texas, but the mother and his children never did.)

▲

Love Letter to My Four Beautiful Daughters,

First, I would like to give honor to God who is the head of my life for blessing my wife and me with four beautiful daughters. Ever since the birth of my first daughter, the first moment I looked at her chubby little face and heard her first cry, I felt a sense of belonging and great responsible. Even if I wanted to hang out with my friends, I couldn't find it in my heart to neglect her.

As a young dad, I was scared at times, however, I was encouraged by my inner feeling of being privileged to bring a new life into the world. Four years later, our union was blessed with my second daughter. My wife and I would work opposite shifts, this way one of us would be home with the girls. Five years later, we were blessed again with our third daughter. At that time, I was very much involved in helping to rise of our children; from giving baths, to changing diapers, calming their cries, reading bedtime stories, to appointments.

By the time my third and fourth daughters were born, I

felt like I was almost a pro at fatherhood. My girls have changed my life as I've learned how to balance time with the Lord, family, work, and me time. Because my daughters are far apart in age, at times I found myself almost being stretched thin. I would take my oldest daughter to compete in pageants, dance competitions, and choir rehearsals, then the other girls to elementary school presentations, track meets, etc. Now that my oldest is in college, she tries her best to help her sisters out which help me greatly.

Growing up in Queens, New York, I was also blessed to have both of my parents at home. However for the most part, as I can remember, my dad was physically and emotionally absent. I would invite him to basketball games, and he would promise me he would come, then I would stare up at the bleachers and he was never there. It was a disappointing feeling, and one of the reasons I promised myself I would be better father to my children. I have had so many priceless memories with my daughters, and it has been such an awesome experience to watch them grow up. Every now and then I look back and pat myself on the back. Don't get me wrong, it wasn't always easy even now because we've had some challenging times.

There are days when I want to pack my bags and get on the first plane to New York, and crawl home to my mother. However, a real man doesn't run away from his responsibilities, and most importantly I wouldn't want another man raising my babies. I realize involvement in my daughters' lives is very important. I may not be the perfect dad, but I tried to provide a loving stable and structured home, and keep my daughters in church. According to the scripture, "We should train a child up in the way he or she would grow and when they are old, they will not depart from it." I also know any man can become a dad, but it takes a real man to be a father.

I hope my daughters will appreciate the love I have for them. Being their dad has also helped me develop and grow as a better dad and better person. I do believe all fathers should love and respect their daughters, in doing so, daughters will see what men think about women. If they strive to be a positive role model in their lives, they may not have the desire to find love in the wrong people. Dads should spend time with their daughters to maintain a father-daughter bond. I often take my daughters on dates to a movie or some activity they like. This is how we get our father-daughter time together.

Finally, I would like to tell my girls they have completed me, and as your dad, I will be there for you. Watching you grow is such an awesome experience for me. If I had to live my life all over again, I wouldn't change a thing.

From your loving and proud father, Jeffrey Morris

▲

Dear Erika,

I can't tell you what an honored and emotional experience it was to walk down the aisle with you at your wedding. There is such a sense of pride in you, and what you have become. Understand it was mixed with a little nervousness that someone will not match up to all we dream a husband should be for you. Your mother and I know how much this relationship will affect you…and your children—either positively or negatively.

Over the years we have worked with many children who didn't have a father in their lives. For some it was a conflict. My heart went out to them. And who will walk them down the aisle? What will they know to look for in a man? I know I'm far from the perfect father. I get too busy and wrapped up in work. It is a good thing your mother makes up for many of my shortfalls. Yet despite those things, I see how important my presence was for our house—not just for you…but for the support, encouragement, and well-being of your mother. When she was at wit's end with three of you little ones running around, I could be the relief valve. When

I was too strict, she could be your comfort. I wish this for every home.

Thank you for letting me dance with you at your reception to the song, "I loved her first." I know I was a bit cold when Nick called me and asked for your hand in marriage. (Be thankful I didn't put him on hold like your sister's husband when he had asked for her hand.) It is a hard thing to imagine "losing" your little daughter. The emotions well up thinking about your birth in the hospital in Providence, Rhode Island; how you would do your dancing and spinning in your slip; how you would express your delightful freedom of thought and expression (like your mom); how you would work alongside me and helped make our house a home. It is nearly impossible to imagine our family life without you.

I'm excited for your life together with Nick. You choose a good man. I'd like to think having a father at home who loved your mother, made you not run into a relationship too quickly to fill a gap in your life, but to take your time to find the kind of man who would be your support and provide a nurturing home for your daughters someday, God willing. I hope he too will have what brings special meaning to a father's life—a daughter to make him proud.

Now, to practice my speech for any young man your younger sister brings home…

Love, your dad, Pastor David A. Kehl

▲

Dear Daughter Tammie,

I know I wasn't there for you when you were a little girl. It was my own fault I missed so many years of your life. I was young, selfish, and foolish when I left you all. So many times I wanted to come back, but as time went on, I was too scared, and didn't think I could be the father you all deserve.

Although I wish the circumstances were different, I am so

glad to be back in your life. I wish I could turn back the time so we could regain the years we have lost.

I am so proud of who you have become, despite of my absent. You are a caring, compassionate, and forgiving woman of God. Thank you for your care, love, and forgiveness. Every day I spend with you, I find myself learning from you, and I have become a better man. It feels so good to be here with you as you care for me because I can't physically care for myself. I owe so much gratitude to you, and I appreciate you for taking care of me better than anyone has ever cared for me.

Love, Your father, Cleo Harris

Dear Daddy,

Thank you for being willing to share. I know it was a tough topic. I want you to know, although you were not in my life growing up, I still love you. While growing up, I felt like you are my only father, and I knew you would one day come back in my life, and you did. I knew one day you will need your children. I thank God for giving me the ability to forgive you, love you, and care for you. I am so blessed to be able to experience the father-daughter love of which I had always dreamed. It is never too late because a girl always needs her father, no matter how old she gets.

I love you daddy, and I know deep down inside, you may feel guilty because of everything. I want you to know you don't need to feel guilty. You are a blessing in my life.

Your daughter, Tammie Harris (See above letter)

▲

Dear Melanie,

On this day you will join over four hundred and fifty of your fellow Carthage College family in walking across the stage to receive your college degree, a journey both fulfilling and challenging.

Watching the commencement ceremony with anxious excitement will be Polly and me, Grandma, and Uncle Brad. And no doubt, walking in spirit beside you on the stage, faces beaming with pride and love, will be your grandpa Bill, great-grandpa Tony, and of course your beloved mother, who will be the proudest of them all!

As I reflect now upon the past twenty-two years, which seemed to have flown by, I share what I am sure are the same feelings most parents have as one of their children reaches this significant milestone. It is a simple question: "Where did all that time go?" Can this be the same little girl who took her first steps while her mom and dad sat on the floor encouraging her, hands outreached, ready to catch her if she stumbled? Can this be the same little girl whose small hand quickly pulled away from mine as she excitedly ran into her 4K classroom for the first time?

It is often said, "It seems like only yesterday," and it is certainly true as I so clearly remember some of those other milestones in your life: Confirmation, the transition from Atonement elementary school to Wisconsin Lutheran High School, and then all too quickly, high school graduation.

As life goes, along with the good times came challenges and heartbreak. The loss of your mom was especially hard on us all, and more recently the loss of Grandpa Bill, whom you shared a very special and close relationship as we were blessed to be living in his home, and then later right across the street from him.

Through those difficulties and others, I encouraged you to stay strong in your faith in God, and to believe He will always dry our tears and heal our wounds. In the good times, I tried to always remind you to be grateful for all blessings, which come from God, and to always remember to put our Lord and Savior ahead of all things.

And in that spirit, I have also encouraged you to always

follow your dreams, and never let anyone tell you, "It cannot be done." Someday you will come to cherish those stories of my life, as well as our talks, when I am no longer around to tell them to you. If you make your goals and dreams centered around Christ, and you persist in them in prayer and action, you can and will achieve anything you set out to do.

So as you complete one journey and set out on a new chapter in your life, my prayer for you continues to be that you trust in God in all you seek and do, pray regularly, praising Him and seeking His guidance, and always make Christ the head of your household and family. In Christ's salvation we are promised a rich eternity together with Him and all our loved ones who have gone before us.

Love always,

Dad *[From Bill Lambrecht to his daughter Melanie Lambrecht]*

CHAPTER 16:

Who Will Fill Those Empty Shoes?

Children of the Lost

Babies born immune to pain, as their mother and father have had nothing to gain.

Young mother's growing beyond her nest with too many to feed at her breast.

Fathers don't stay long enough to see who was left behind or who they grow up to be.

Mothers are left alone indeed with no stable home and much in need.

Little minds trying hard to understand why Mama keeps chasing after that abusive man.

The man who drains her to her soul, beats her, and leaves her alone in the cold.

Sons grow up with destructive minds, no knowledge of love in the darkest times.

Gangs and guns become his friends, while his little sister runs into a predator's hands.

They learn how to do themselves in; no daddy to teach them other than Mama's many men.

Many are dying at our feet, from deadly battles within our streets.

We are losing them at every cost. How can we help save the children of the lost?

A few days after I had finished writing this last chapter, my brother called, saying Oprah had done a show called "Fatherless Sons." I was floored because my brother (who's also fatherless) had recently began his own journey of healing from fatherlessness. As we shared our personal experiences, I discovered the many layers of the effects of fatherlessness. Soon I became overwhelmed by passion and decided to form an advocacy to expose the devastating effects of fatherlessness that many suffering from fatherlessness learn to mask.

I started writing my book two years prior to this show. However, when Oprah did the episode, "Daddyless Daughters," it confirmed it was time for me to become transparent and expose my hidden pain. These shows couldn't have come at a better time because they helped create the awareness and reality about such a tender topic. Although watching Oprah helped validate my epiphany, it was more heartfelt that my brother was able to realize he, too, was not alone. Not only has my brother felt the loss of his identity, he also felt abandoned and unworthy.

I thank God for giving us the courage to face the fatherless epidemic together. I take my hat off to him because he is now a father who is well aware of the love and validation his daughter needs. Some people think I wanted him on the cover of my book because he was my handsome younger brother. The truth is, I often watch in amazement as he adores his little princess. When I am around them, I could feel the amount of love and passion he holds for his daughter. I knew this father-daughter image would capture the hearts of people, like it has captured mine.

It's no secret: Boys who grow up without fathers, tend to repeat the cycle by becoming fathers who abandon their children. However, my brother like many others, found the courage to love his daughter even when he felt unloved, stay with her even when he felt abandoned, and validate her even when he felt unworthy. My brother has never seen his father, and was conceived by his mother who was receiving care in a mental health hospital. I greatly respect him for having the courage to accept his truth, and loving anyway. He is not perfect, but he is determined to interrupt the cycle of fatherlessness within our family system.

The reality of it all has forced me to be honest about my own three young boys, who are growing up without their father. In the past I carried guilt because he was not involved in their lives as much as he should be. Although he is now sometimes physically present when he stops in for a short visit here and there, he really doesn't have the tools he needs to be emotionally available. Because of our family dynamics, a no-contact order was set in place several years ago to prevent him from having unsupervised interactions with them. At the time this order was necessary to cure the chaos and disorder he caused in my home in the past. However, I came to realize it would better benefit my sons if I helped him find the support he needed to be a good father. This was tough, because we didn't have the best history, there were issues with respecting boundaries, and the communication between us was even worse. However, I knew I needed to forgive him so we could move forward and parent our sons.

I knew even if I were the best mother in the world, I would never replace the role of their father. Before I had tried to fool myself into thinking if I put them in the best schools, keep them in church, be the funniest and coolest mom ever, they wouldn't realize they needed a dad. *Wrong! Wrong! Wrong!* As they got older, they began to long for an interaction with him, and needed him as much as I needed my own father. In spite of the no-contact order against him, I reached out to him and made a commitment to helping him get back in his boys' lives. I love my boys, and I didn't want to allow them to continue the cycle of fatherlessness. I knew this would be a generational curse that could lead them to the heartbreaking reality of abandoning their own children. The motive was no longer me waiting for him to fail so the door was closed, but to do all I could to help him succeed, and keep the door open.

I didn't know where to start, but I went on my search to find out what was available in my community. I started by Googling fatherhood organizations, parenting groups for fathers, agencies providing mediation, etc. I also searched nationwide and even wrote a letter to President Obama. More was available than I had ever imagined, for example, the National Fathers' Initiative, the local office in Milwaukee, Wisconsin, and many other fatherhood programs who helped fathers have a more active parenting role. I contacted them, and also initiated the mediation counseling ordered by the courts in order to have visitation his reinstated. I continue to look for opportunities to include their father in their lives. It is still a work in progress, but things continue to progress little by little.

Over the last year, I interviewed so many of these organizations' leaders because I wanted to establish my new role as an advocate for fatherhood. I also wanted to find out what services were available not only for my sons' father, but for fathers who I came across in my private practice. I was on a mission, and my purpose was to be an advocate for the many children I come in contact with within my community. I wasn't exactly sure where my place or purpose was, but I knew it had something to do with helping fathers reconnect with their children.

I know I can't expect changes overnight, and I am aware programs out there are doing their best to make a difference. However, I think the problem has gotten so big it will take an even greater impact from community leaders before we can begin to see the change. Not a night goes by when I am not reminded of the violence occurring within the urban community. It seems like young teens in the inner city of Milwaukee are shot almost every night. Most often it is the young people who have no fathers' presences to teach them their value. I have had contact with many of those kids while working in the school district. It saddens me that a young teenage boy is not able to see his life beyond the gates of his youth. How then can he worry about being a father?

While visiting New Orleans and taking a morning walk, I came upon a strange encounter. A young man approached me as I was returning to my hotel. I was startled because I wasn't aware of his presence, yet a voice inside of me told me to remain calm. He appeared clueless as he handed me his card, and said he was the manager at a tattoo shop a few blocks away. He had no way of knowing I had been thinking about covering up a tattoo I had acquired in New Orleans five years ago when I was on vacation with my ex-fiancé. This tattoo reminded me of the broken woman I was in my past. Although I felt awkward, I agreed I would come in later in the afternoon. I handed him one of my flyers, which gave a brief description of my upcoming book.

Before I returned to my hotel, I watched him walk away, and noticed he stared down at the picture on the flyer. Later I went to the tattoo shop as I promised, and inquired about the cover-up. I did not expect the welcoming I received when I entered. It was as if they were waiting for my arrival. I quickly noticed several other men there, all of whom were intrigued by the flyer, and wanted to know more about the book. I gave a little presentation, and before I realized it, I was conducting an informal panel discussion on fatherhood. I wish I had been better prepared so it could have been recorded. However, nonetheless I asked for a pen and paper, and jotted down as much of the conversation I could.

The men included three white men, and four black men, ranging in the ages from 23 to 49. All of them admitted to having young children they had not seen in quite some time, and several of them said they had more than one "Baby Mama." I had often wondered what barriers prevented fathers from staying connected to their children after they ended the relationship with the "Baby Mamma." Surprisingly, now I was being given the opportunity. I asked the questions as they came to mind.

Below is a list of reasons these fathers stated why they haven't see their children, and why they had emotionally abandoned them:

> **1.** The baby mama interferes with them and their child's relationship. "She always finds a way of putting herself in the middle. Most men want to see their kids, and when they don't, it's usually about the woman, not the kids."

2. Most men can't handle the baby mama drama. They would be there if she allowed him to just be a daddy to his kids. "She is still stuck on why we broke up, and often uses the kids as pawns. If you going over there with her, my baby ain't going with you."

3. Some men are afraid of the responsibility because no one ever told them how to be a daddy. "Most of us don't have fathers ourselves."

4. Most men are afraid of the system, and feel it doesn't support fathers who want to pursue joint custody or have fatherhood rights. "A lot of us are afraid we will go to jail because of child support. She threatens to put us on papers." (Some men fear being adjudicated because of their misconception of their rights in the court system, like fathers who want to have joint custody.)

5. They don't want their kids caught up in the middle, or have to choose. "I had assumed kids are better off with a mama, and could get along well without a daddy."

6. They fear they are not good enough because they don't have anything to offer their children. "If you don't have no job, you can't do nothing for them, and the old girl ain't gonna want you coming around with nothing."

7. Some fathers don't have a role model around to learn from. "There is no one there to tell you that you have to father your kids. If you don't have anyone to show you, sometimes you just don't know."

8. The court system favors the mom, and assumes she is the most suitable caregiver, even when she's not. "My baby mama was gone for six months, and I was taking care of the kids by myself. When she decided to come back, she took them from school and moved them out of state with her. I tried to fight for them, but was told there was nothing I could do, so I gave up and haven't seen my kids in two years."

9. Some fathers are emotionally disconnected and think they are being good fathers because they send money, and call every now and then. "I thought if I help provide financial support and call once and awhile, I was doing what I needed to do. I didn't realize I needed to be there."

10. Some fathers have their own painful issues. "Sometimes you have a lot going on, and you get so caught up in yourself you don't think about what the kids need."

At the end of our discussion, I asked the men if there was anything they wanted me to mention to women in the book—things they really wanted women to know.

This is what they had to say:

- Women should appreciate when a man wants to be in his kids' lives instead of trying to keep him away.
- Women should keep the kids out of the middle, and give them the freedom to love their daddies, too.
- Women should stop bad-mouthing them in front of their kids.
- Women should stop trying to play the daddy role, and stop telling the kids you are their mama and daddy, because you are not.
- Women should deal with your personal baggage, and move on.

This impromptu discussion in the tattoo shop gave me so much insight, and I was also able to have an impact on them. Two of the men called their children while I was there, one of the men wrote a letter to his daughters for my book, and the others said they were going to think about how they were going to reach out to their children. Toward the end of our conversation, many of the men wanted to know how to get over the guilt, reach out to their children, and forgive themselves for allowing so much time to pass. I felt honored to have had the opportunity to listen to all of their stories, and give advice.

Who Will Fill Those Empty Shoes?

The young man who had followed me earlier admitted he had watched me walk by, and waited for me to walk back because a voice spoke to him, telling him he needed to talk to me. He said he had followed me for three or four blocks, and didn't know why he felt the urge to speak to me, or what he would say when he came in contact with me. This sounds weird, but I believe God had his hands in this, because this young man hadn't seen his baby girls in a while, and after writing a letter for my book, he called them. I left there feeling like I was on cloud nine, and I was thanking God for the experience.

However, the next morning God allowed me to encounter someone with an opposing point-of-view. On my last day there, my friend and I decided to tour the French Quarter. We came upon a nice, little cozy restaurant and decided to stop. Before I knew it, I was engaged in a conversation about my book with two men working there. One of these men challenged my theory, and said I didn't know what I was talking about. He then went on to proclaim he had nothing to with how his twenty-two-year-old daughter had turned out. This was despite the fact she was eight when he went to prison for twelve years for a charge he did not disclose. He said when he got out, she was twenty, but during the last two years their relationship had been rocky.

When I asked why he felt it was so rocky, he replied, "Because she ain't nothing but a lazy b____ who sat on her butt doing nothing but having baby after baby, and waiting for these men to take care of her." I was taken aback by his comments and asked if he thought his going to prison had anything to do with who his daughter was. He got very offended, responding, "She understood why I went to prison. We had a level of understanding, and it was up to her mother to look after her." Before I realized it, I found myself in a heated argument because of my desire to defend her. By now this man was standing over me, in my face, and coming at me really strong. I was shaking and almost in tears but I stood my ground. When I realized it was a dead end debate, I got up and left the restaurant.

This encounter was shocking but necessary for it was the first time I realized that every absent father would not be willing to receive my message. On a much closer level, this man's resistance reminded me I still had unresolved issues with my own father. Like my father, he was putting the responsibility of raising his daughter solely on her mother and/or herself.

After returning home, I looked to my community for answers. Instead of being angry about my encounter, I wanted to know why this man had reacted in such a way. It was important I speak with someone who had experience working with absent dads. I once again reached out to the Prison Action Milwaukee (PAM) re-entry program, and also Mr. Holmes from My Father's House INC. My Father's House INC, helps local fathers reestablish their rights as fathers, resolve child support and visitation concerns, and provide parenting resources.

This time I insisted we sit down and I conducted an interview with both organizations. Although I felt both interviews were very resourceful, it was the interview with MFH most relevant for the chapter.

Below is a transcript of my interview questions, and his responses.

1. What do absent fathers say are the major reasons they remain absent?

- Some fathers feel if they do not have a job to financially provide for their children, they have nothing to give.
- Some fathers are afraid, and just don't know how.
- Some fathers get caught up in their new relationship, and have other children, and don't want that to threaten his current situation.
- Some of the things he did in the past prevented him from coming back to his children. Sometimes it is too hard for him to acknowledge that person from the past.

Who Will Fill Those Empty Shoes?

- Fathers can lack the nurturing for their children. Unlike mothers who have the innate ability to nurture, fathers have to learn it.

2. What percentage of fathers you work with come in by choice?

"The majority of fathers come in on their own by word of mouth, legal advice, and child support concerns. We are not court ordered."

3. How does your organization get absent fathers to buy in?

"Some of the fathers get involved in support groups, and we also reach out to some fathers at community events, health fair, festivals, etc."

4. What kind of support do you offer to assure fathers remain present?

"We make ourselves available 24/7 with those who show interest in turning things around. We are there for them, and we have access to the system. We make sure our fathers are prepared to be involved as a full-time father. If not, we encourage visitation."

5. How do you measure your success rates?

"We are getting prepared to put things in place so there is a way to measure the success."

6. In addition to the reunification piece, what other services are available?

"Parenting classes, 13-week groups, father nurturing programs for fathers in prison, 24/7 Dad, InsideOut Dad, staff training programs, career assessments, counseling services, employment skills, and soft skills."

7. Are there any programs for single mothers to help them support their children's father so they continue to be engaged fathers?

"Understand that a father's role is important. There are currently no programs for women, but there are programs open to the public, and women are welcome to come and get involved."

8. Why did you get involved with the My Father's House, INC Organization?

"Because I was very engaged with my own children. They were like my second chance, and I didn't want them to grow up without me. The more involved I became with them, the more I realized it was a duty as a father. I wanted other fathers in the community to understand how important his role is. This is why the Daddy Daughter Dance we do every year is so important to me. Fathers go way out for this event, and they are so proud when they come in with their daughters."

As I close this final chapter, I realize I am so eager to find ways to be productive so I can help facilitate the circle of healing from generation to generation. I hope this chapter is full of resources, and can begin to help repair broken communities. I am a firm believer if we plant a seed, it will continue to grow. I will continue to travel one city at a time until my voice is heard, my story is heard, and my purpose is complete. I realize I am only one person, and everyone may not receive my message. However, if I can touch one father, one daughter, one son, it affirms I am doing my work. I pledge to be active in advocating for fatherhood, motherhood, and healthy families.

My Epiphany

A few years ago I had no idea I would have written a book, faced my childhood abandonment, and become passionate about the effects of fatherlessness. As I began to heal, my pain turned into a passion, which has driven me to advocacy, public speaking, and healing the fatherless generation.

I couldn't simply write a letter to my absent father, resolve my personal problems, and then move on with my life. Nope, that was not God's plan, at least not his plan for me. If you knew me back then, you would not believe I am the same woman I am today. I would have never admitted to myself or anyone else I was fatherless. However, the last encounter with my father sent me on a spiraling journey with twist and turns leading to my truth. Not only did I find healing, I realized the fatherlessness epidemic was *much bigger than me*.

As I continued my own soul searching, it became real to me—being fatherless played a huge part in how I felt about myself, loved myself, and expected to be treated by others. The more I sought answers for myself, the more passionate I became about finding answers for others. Soon I realized it was more than me telling my story, I realized God was working on me so I would be prepared for my purpose. I became curious about the current issues our communities faced, and I began to see the root was most often somehow connected to fatherlessness. Who would have known God would use my pain for his glory, and my benefit?

As I continued to be obedient and listened to God's direction, I relied on him to lead my every step. Every day I look for an opportunity to share my story, with the hopes of helping other people heal. I realized I have become very passionate about the topic, and the more I speak, the more confident I become about my cause and purpose. I am determined to impact the world as I set to fulfill my destiny. I believe one day I will be standing before large groups of brokenhearted people helping them implement their own journeys of healing.

Getting to this point was an amazing process, because I did not wake up and feel an instant change. No one had the ability to pull me out of where I was. Although many were there listening and supporting me, I can't give anyone credit but him. When I thought I could not do it, and was about to give up, God sent many messages to me through so many different sources. When I finally stopped hiding and listened, it was like he promised. Yes, I wept a little bit along the way, but God was with me. It was truly God's gift that allowed me to stay strong and keep going even when the odds were against me. As he guided me through my transformation, I came out of my cocoon and became a beautiful butterfly.

As I continue progressing along my journey, I am still shocked, because I never believed I would be here feeling so free. It feels like a heavy weight has been lifted from me, and suddenly I can move about with ease. I no longer carry the weight of my mask.

About the Author

Sonja P. Moore currently resides in Milwaukee, Wisconsin. As a young child, she was always interested in writing, and has used it as a way of expressing difficult emotional. She has a Bachelor's degree in Psychology, a Master's degree in Educational Psychology, a Post-Master's Certification in Marriage & Family Therapy, and will pursue her PHD in Marriage and Family Therapy in the fall of 2014. She has over fourteen years of service as a school counselor in Wisconsin's largest urban school district, and over six years as a practicing psychotherapist. In previous years, she has worked in many other community organizations, including treatment centers, group homes, and social service agencies. She has also developed therapeutic material for support groups, married couples, and parenting groups.

While in the school district, she continues to service the high-risk population affected by fatherlessness, poverty, violence, low achievement, teen pregnancy, homelessness, etc. In addition, Sonja is also co-owner of Changing Dynamics Marriage & Family Therapy, LLC, a family therapy practice in Milwaukee that aims to restore broken relationships within families. As a psychotherapist and school counselor, she helps her clients and students get to the root issues that interrupt their emotional well-being. She is passionate about the work she does, and wants to continue to make an impact on the community.

Letter from President Obama:

I was driven by passion and needed to do something so wrote to everyone that I could think of, including the president. Surprisingly, he wrote back.

THE WHITE HOUSE
WASHINGTON

January 27, 2014

Ms. Sonja Moore-Hazelwood
Milwaukee, Wisconsin

Dear Sonja:

    Thank you for writing. I have heard from single parents across America about the challenges they face, and I am glad you reached out to me to share your perspective.

    Single parents do a heroic job raising their children, tirelessly balancing work and family. They often spend long hours on the job and make tremendous sacrifices to provide the time and care their children need. Today's economic climate further intensifies the difficulties these families feel every day.

    I know the struggles and opportunities that single parents experience because I was raised by a single mother. She provided unending support and guidance, and I know that, like her, single parents across our country are working to help their children achieve their dreams.

    My Administration is working hard to lend a hand to single parents. The American Recovery and Reinvestment Act has invested in child support enforcement and provides more than $4 billion to increase enrollment in Head Start, Early Head Start, and other child-care programs. The Recovery Act also created the Making Work Pay Tax Credit and the American Opportunity Tax Credit, which help parents make ends meet and pay for higher education. Looking forward, I am working on investing in high-quality early childhood education and advancing flexible work policies to help parents care for their children. Assistance with financing education can be found at www.StudentAid.Ed.gov and www.Opportunity.gov.

    Communities and government can also work together to encourage responsible parenting. For example, I have begun a national conversation on fatherhood to explore how we can encourage fathers to fulfill their responsibilities and serve as positive role models. All of us must work together—moms, dads, community organizations, and all levels of government—to strengthen our Nation's families. I invite you to join this discussion by raising these issues in your community.

    For additional information about assistance for families with children, please visit www.ACF.gov and www.Fatherhood.gov. Thank you, again, for writing.

Sincerely,

Barack Obama

MILWAUKEE'S 11th ANNUAL
DADDY/DAUGHTER DANCE
Sponsored by Milwaukee Public Schools
North Division High School, Milwaukee, Wisconsin
"It was a great turn out and daughters of all ages attended
with their dad's".

www.ingramcontent.com/pod-product-compliance
Lightning Source LLC
Chambersburg PA
CBHW071658090426
42738CB00009B/1576